Sitting on the Rainbow

and 58 other Kids Sermons from the Gospel of Mark

Ruth Gilmore

Augsburg Books

MINNEAPOLIS

To Bruce and Marta Boyce
with love and thanks

SITTING ON THE RAINBOW
and 58 Other Kids Sermons from the Gospel of Mark

Cover design by Marti Naughton
Cover graphics by EyeWire
Book design by Michelle L. N. Cook

Library of Congress Cataloging-in-Publication Data
Gilmore, Ruth, 1962-
    Sitting on the rainbow: and 58 other kids sermons from the Gospel of Mark / by Ruth Gilmore.
        p.cm.
    ISBN 0-8066-4081-2 (alk. paper)
    1. Children's sermons. 2. Bible. N.T. Mark—Sermons. I. Title.
    BV4315.G393 2002
    252'.53—dc21   2002023227

The paper used in this publication meets the minimum requirements of American National Standard for Information Sciences—Permanence of Paper for Printed Library Materials, ANSI Z329.48-1984. ♾ ™

Manufactured in the U.S.A.

06   05   5   6   7   8   9   10

Contents

Sunday	Theme	

Foreword
by Walter Wangerin, Jr.

Ruth Gilmore has gathered together bright, brief patterns for communicating core truths of lessons in the Revised Common Lectionary.

As worship itself engages more than half our senses, so sound, sight, touch, motion, discovery, delight—oh, and the near presence of the storyteller—all draw children, Sunday by Sunday, chapter by chapter, into the one real story of our salvation.

Here are little stories. Here are suggestions for tactile interactions. Here are frameworks for your own personal stories.

But the proclamation itself waits for you—and for the dramatic moment when you engage the senses, the fierce interest, and the hearts of the children.

Two things only will fill Gilmore's bright patterns with the power of a living Lord, and both things are called by the same name: love.

If you love the Lord of the story with your entire being, your telling will find its most persuasive style, your style, the manner you use when there's nothing more important to tell another soul than this. In you, the story will flare and live— and you, your presence and your person, will become the manifest evidence of it.

And if you love the children arrayed before you, you'll tell that story and shape it and design it specifically for them. You'll watch them, and they'll see the personal invitation in your eyes. You'll be alert to their tiniest gestures and their attentions. You will rejoice when the story goes home to their hearts, and they will see your joy, and their delight will grow the keener.

This is the invitation in these pieces by Ruth Gilmore: an invitation to proclamation.

Accept the invitation with love!

Introduction

"Let the little children come to me, and do not hinder them, for the kingdom of God belongs to such as these" (Matt. 19:14 NIV). Jesus' words remind us to see a child through the eyes of God—not as a noisy distraction from business at hand, but as an honored inheritor of God's kingdom and a model of humility. Children, dancing their way through life, not yet filled with pride and self, still delightfully saturated with the joy of living—they embrace the kingdom. They live in the moment of grace.

This book offers fifty-nine chances to interact with children during a year of worship services. Children's time is a magical moment in the church service. When young ones are invited forward, many will spring from their seats and gallop to the front of the church, thrilled to sit next to you and have the attention of the whole congregation. And the idea of hearing a good story told just for them, or the chance to unravel the meaning of an intriguing object lesson—well, these are opportunities just too good to pass up.

So, right from the start, all the advantages belong to you.

Stories have power.
Even as you capture the children's attention, adults in the congregation will be drawn into the story, hearing Bible truths told in a new way, appreciating the simplicity you have brought to the message. We are—all of us—children, the sons and daughters of our heavenly Parent. Jesus reaches out to the child in each of us, teaching through stories and parables, because children love a good story.

The sermons in this book ask you to be a storyteller. Each one is self-contained and ready to use. But before you begin, here are tips to sharpen your storytelling skills and make these children's sermons the most effective they can be.

Sitting on the Rainbow

Use sermons that work for you.

If you are following the Revised Common Lectionary, you will find that each sermon is based on one of the texts for the day. There are fifty-nine sermons in all—a year's worth of sermons, plus seven extras (for non-Sunday events or festivals). If you are not following a lectionary, you can search the contents list by theme to find applicable sermons.

Build relationships.

Many sermons in this book make use of a personal anecdote or illustration. Children love to hear real-life stories about their elders, especially if they like the elders who are telling the stories. The relationship with your listeners has a lot to do with the connection you build in your first moments with them. It is important to be on their level—physically as well as intellectually. Sit with the children and recognize the importance of each child with your gestures and eye contact. Make it clear that you are eager to travel into the story with them.

And it's good to remember that our preconceived ideas about teaching and learning may be wrong. Even though we might want our listeners to sit quietly and keep their eyes glued on us, some children learn best while in motion. Some of my most active listeners often turn out to be the ones who most fully understand the point I am trying to make.

Keep it simple, brief, concrete.

I have tried to keep the language of these sermons simple and direct, easily understandable to a child. Most sermons will take five minutes or less to deliver. A child's attention is a tenuous and precious thing. Children are intent on soaking in every miracle of the world around them, and to concentrate on one thing at a time is a considerable challenge.

Many sermons make use of a simple object to illustrate a lesson. (A brief note at the beginning of each sermon will alert you to any special preparations or props.) Children will

understand and retain more as more of their five senses are engaged. Their sense of touch or smell or taste will draw them back into the sermon and remind them of the truth that was taught. And with God's grace, they will learn that truth by heart.

Make the sermons your own—the CD-ROM.
As was noted earlier, these sermons can be used just as they are—read directly from the page. *But they will be even better with a bit of preparation and personalization.* Use the enclosed CD to customize each sermon for the most appropriate delivery in your situation, for your audience. Add or substitute your own interesting, relevant stories wherever possible. Build in anecdotes, illustrations, names from your congregation, city, or community.

Prepare.
It's always better to tell your sermon than to read it. The more familiar you are with the sermon, the easier it will be to *talk* to your listeners. In a well-rehearsed play, the trappings of the performance fade into the background while the emotion and meaning of the play comes into focus. A performer who knows the part well is able to ad-lib if occasion demands.

And while you are sharing your sermons, don't be surprised if a kid puts his or her oar in. That may shift your direction slightly; but if you're prepared, you can go with the flow while continuing to steer gently. The bank you end up traveling to may be more interesting and important than the place you originally were headed.

Visit our Web site, too!
If you have a Web browser, helpful information and resources about children's sermons are available at <www.kidsermons.com>. There you'll be able to contact the

author, read anecdotes, download scripts for puppet shows, find information about other books in the series, and access links to other helpful sites on the Internet. The Web site has an on-line index of all currently available kids sermons by Ruth Gilmore. They are listed by biblical reference in order from the Old Testament to the New Testament.

Finally, enjoy the rewards.

God has generously blessed me through the children who have sat with me on the steps of the altar. I marvel to see how young children can catch the meaning behind stories before I've even gotten to the explanations. I rejoice in the delightful insights of my young audience. I suspect that, through the years, the children have taught me far more than I have taught them.

May God bless you as you teach the children—and, in teaching them, welcome the Lord Jesus himself into your midst.

A Sharp Lookout

Preparation: Prepare a volunteer to provide a distraction at the appropriate time during the children's sermon.

Today is the first Sunday in Advent. *(You may, at this time, take note of the Advent wreath and other Advent decorations.)* Advent is a time of waiting and getting ready for the arrival of Jesus at Christmas, but it is also a time when we think about watching and waiting for Jesus to come again.

Jesus told his disciples very plainly that he was going to return to earth again, but he did not tell them exactly when that would happen. Jesus said that only the Father in heaven knows the exact time. Jesus explained that his return to earth could be compared to a man who left to go on a trip and told his workers what to do while he was gone, but did not tell them when he was coming back. In the Gospel of Mark, chapter 13, Jesus said, "Keep a sharp lookout! For you do not know when the homeowner will return—at evening, midnight, early dawn, or late daybreak. What I say to you I say to everyone: Watch for his return!" (vv. 35–37 NLT).

Can anyone tell me what it means to keep a sharp lookout? *(Let children respond.)* You keep a sharp lookout when you watch carefully for something. If you are the lookout, do you have to pay close attention? Do you have to keep awake and alert? *(Children may answer.)* How many of you are good lookouts? Raise your hand if you think you could keep a sharp lookout.

Well, I have a test for you. I'm going to go out that door *(indicate a nearby exit)*, and I will return through that door. I want everyone to keep a sharp lookout and have your eyes on that door when I come back. Can you do that? I might come back right away, or it may be a little longer, but don't take your eyes off that door. *(You exit and soon after, the "distraction" enters from the opposite direction with a yo-yo or ball, etc. You may return while children are distracted.)*

Hello! I'm back! How many of you were still watching the door when I entered? *(Pause for response.)* Sometimes it can be very hard to keep a sharp lookout, especially when there are other things trying to get your attention. This world is full of distractions, especially as we get close to Christmas. There are decorations and toys and cookies and so many things that keep us from watching and waiting for Jesus. During this season of Advent, let's try to keep our eyes on the reason for the season. Keep a sharp lookout for Jesus!

Dear Jesus, as we wait for your return, help us to keep our eyes on you. We want to be doing the things that you want us to do while we are waiting.

Notes

God's Hug

Preparation: You may want to ask adult volunteers to help you with the big group hug at the end of the sermon.

It's the second Sunday in Advent, isn't it? During Advent, we wait for the coming of Jesus at Christmas. Sometimes it feels like we have to wait for a long time. If you have ever waited a long time for your mom or dad to get home and you've been missing them, you might feel sad and want to be comforted. What happens when you finally see each other again? How would your mom or dad give you comfort? *(Let children respond.)* Do they wrap their arms around you? It feels good when we can get a hug from someone. A hug is a real comfort to us when we've been waiting for someone.

There's a verse in the Old Testament book of Isaiah that says, "Comfort, comfort my people . . . speak tenderly. . . . [The Lord] will feed his flock like a shepherd. He will carry the lambs in his arms, holding them close to his heart. He will gently lead the mother sheep with their young" (Isa. 40:1–2, 11 NLT).

When Isaiah says, "He will gather the lambs in his arms," who do you think those lambs are? *(Wait for answer.)* You are God's lambs, and he is your shepherd. When you're lonely or sad, God wants to take you in his arms and comfort you. But sometimes we can't feel God's hugs. So who can God use to give us hugs for him? *(Children may respond.)* Yes, we get hugs from our parents, our brothers and sisters, and friends—we get hugs from people who care about us.

Do you think God is big enough to hug the whole world? Yes, God is big enough to hold all of his lambs at one time. How many people can you hug at once? Can you get your arms around just one person at a time, or can you hug two people at once? If your arms were really long, you could maybe hug three or four people at once.

I know I can hug at least one person. I'll show you, if someone would volunteer to be hugged. *(Give one volunteer a hug.)* And I'm pretty sure that I can hug two people at once. *(Give two volunteers a hug.)* But in order to hug all of you at once, the way our Father in heaven can, I will need some help. *(Have your volunteer adults come forward to help out.)* Now let's see if we can give all of God's lambs a hug at the same time, the way God can. *(Give a group hug.)*

That was a very big hug, wasn't it? Remember that God is bigger than any sadness or loneliness, and he can comfort all of us, but he needs people to help him give hugs. Will you remember to give out plenty of hugs today? After our prayer, you can go back to your places and give someone a hug.

We thank you, our Lord and Comforter, that you care about us and want to hold us close. Help us to show others your love.

Notes

Make a Path

Preparation: Bring several large squares of wrapping paper, a fat marker, and a bag for garbage.

Today is the third Sunday in Advent. Christmas might still seem a long way off, but while we wait, we should be getting ready. How do people get ready for Christmas? *(Let children respond. Note the "getting ready" suggestions, writing several on the back of each sheet of wrapping paper. Then throw the papers on the floor in front of you.)* We get ready for Christmas by making lists of things to do and things to buy. We get ready by wrapping presents. We have parties and get dressed up. We send out Christmas cards. We do Christmas baking. *(A pile of paper should be growing at your feet.)*

There are so many busy things to do at Christmastime, that sometimes we forget who we are supposed to be getting ready for. Christmas celebrates the coming of someone very important. Who is that? *(Children may answer.)* Yes! Christmas celebrates the birth of Jesus. Jesus is coming! And during Advent we are supposed to be getting ready to receive Jesus.

Before Christmas comes, we are busy getting ready in many ways, but the most important thing we can do is to get our hearts ready to receive Jesus. John the Baptist was a man whose job was to help people get ready for the coming of Jesus. He knew what he was supposed to do. When people asked him who he was, John the Baptist answered, "I am a voice shouting in the wilderness, 'Prepare a straight pathway for the Lord's coming!'"(John 1:23 NLT).

If the Lord were to come down this aisle and walk right up to us, would he have a straight pathway? *(Indicate the mess of paper on the floor.)* No, he'd have to make a path through all of these busy things that we do to get ready for Christmas. Can you help make a straight pathway through the middle of all this? Let's make a straight pathway for Jesus. *(Children can help push wrapping aside to make a path down the middle.)* Thank you. Now Jesus has a pathway.

Advent is an exciting time of getting ready for Christmas, but in the middle of all of our busyness, we need to remember to make a straight pathway in our hearts so Jesus can come in. Before you go, can each of you grab a paper and put it in the bag? Then you can find your pathway back to your seats.

Lord Jesus, come into our hearts in the middle of our Christmas preparations and remind us to make a pathway for you. Help us to receive you with joy.

Notes

Nothing Is Impossible

Preparation: Bring a doll wrapped in swaddling clothes to represent Jesus.

Today is the fourth Sunday in Advent. Christmas is very near. In the middle of all the busyness and decorations and excitement about presents, are you remembering who we are getting ready for? What is Christmas all about? *(Let children respond.)* That's right, we're waiting for the baby Jesus. This is not an ordinary baby; this is the Son of God. When this baby comes, incredible things will happen.

Now I know that you are never supposed to bring dangerous weapons to church, but in my bag, I have a model of an extremely powerful and dangerous weapon. What do you think it could be? *(Let children guess.)* This weapon has already been used here on earth. It was used to save all of us. And it broke down the gates of hell and destroyed the devil's power. *(Retrieve baby Jesus doll and show everyone.)*

You wouldn't normally think of a baby as a dangerous weapon, would you? Babies are helpless and soft and sweet. What could a little baby do? But baby Jesus was no ordinary baby. In sending Jesus to earth, God did the impossible. Is it possible for the power of God to be contained within a tiny infant? It happened. Could God love us so much that he would send his only son to save us from our sins? It happened. Could God, as a human, take on all the powers of the devil and sin and destroy that power with love? It happened. With God, nothing is impossible.

Sitting on the Rainbow

When the angel Gabriel appeared to Mary and told her that she was going to give birth to God's Son, it was hard for Mary to believe. The angel told Mary, "Nothing is impossible with God" (Luke 1:37 NLT). A wonderful song by an English composer named Benjamin Britten describes Baby Jesus as a weapon who came to destroy evil. Britten's song tells how tiny Jesus—just a few days old and shivering in the cold— made the Devil and all the powers of hell shake with fear. Without any weapons or armor, Jesus surprised "the gates of hell" and defeated Satan.

A tiny baby can change the whole world. The power of evil is destroyed by a tiny baby. The baby Jesus comes this Christmas to save us all. The baby Jesus is the Son of God; and with God, nothing is impossible.

Praise to you, Lord God, for sending your only son, Jesus, to our earth as a little baby. Thank you for sending Jesus to save us from our sins and to bring us eternal life!

Notes

The Power of Light

Preparation: Bring a flashlight or a candle. Arrange with the ushers to turn off the lights at the appropriate time.

It's Christmas Eve! It's a wonderful and magical time. On Christmas Eve, we make our final preparations for the arrival of the Christ Child. Jesus, the Light of the world, is coming! In the weeks before Christmas, there are many reminders that the Light is coming. People string lights around their houses, we light the candles on the Advent wreath, around the world people light lanterns, and luminaries line the pathways to house and church.

(Here you may add your own descriptions of the symbolic use of lights at Christmas. My example follows.) I remember when I was a little girl on Christmas Eve, Mother would decorate the Christmas tree with real candles. Then the family would file into the living room singing and see that glorious tree with all of its glowing lights, and we would all gasp! The tree was a reminder of Jesus, the beautiful Light of the world.

Thousands of years ago, before Jesus was born, the prophet Isaiah told the Israelites that a special light was coming. Isaiah said, "The people who walked in darkness have seen a great light; those who lived in a land of deep darkness—on them has light shined" (Isa. 9:2 NRSV). In much of our world today, even the darkest nights are lit up with street lamps and house lights and car headlights. So our "darkness" often isn't as dark as that in Isaiah's world. But even so, when we *are* in the dark, one light can make a difference.

Now I want everyone to quietly hold someone's hand and try to sit very still while the ushers switch off the lights. We're going to pretend that we are the people who live in the land of deep darkness. *(Lights off.)* Now that it's dark, let's see what a difference one light makes. *(Light candle or flashlight.)*

Jesus comes at Christmas as the light to the people in the dark. And even though we modern people have our electric lights and flashlights and streetlights, we are all born in the darkness of sin. Jesus, the Light of the world, comes to push back the darkness of sin, to shine so brightly in our lives that there is not the tiniest bit of dark sin left.

As the ushers turn the lights back on, I invite you to open your hearts to the coming of Jesus, the Light of the world, while we pray together.

Dear Jesus, our Savior, thank you for coming into the world as the great Light. Thank you for pushing back the darkness of our sin and surrounding us with the warmth and healing light of your presence. We praise you for Christmas, Lord. Help us to celebrate your glory.

Notes

Shouting Shepherds

Preparation: Bring a picture of a shepherd's staff, or, if possible, a life-size model of a staff. A picture of a bishop or other church official holding a ceremonial staff may also be used. You may also bring shepherd staff-shaped candy canes to hand out.

A very Merry Christmas to you! Are you happy that Christmas is finally here? *(Let children respond.)* Have you heard people call out to each other, "Merry Christmas!"? That is a wonderful sound to my ears. Merry Christmas! Did you ever wonder what the very first Christmas greeting sounded like? Now people send Christmas greetings with cards or phone calls or even e-mail, but they also still call out to each other, "Merry Christmas!"

Who do you suppose were the very first people to shout out the news that Jesus was born? *(Children may answer.)* The very first people to shout out the good news that Jesus was born were shepherds. The angels told them where to find Jesus, and they ran to the stable and saw the Son of God lying in a manger. They knew right away that this was important news and they told everyone who would listen about the baby Jesus.

Those shepherds were the first preachers. They told everyone the good news. They couldn't keep quiet. The shepherds were probably not used to speaking out in public, and they were certainly not used to having people listen to them. In those days, shepherds usually did not have much education. They couldn't read or write. They might never have gone to church. But God sent the angels to the shepherds.

They were the first to hear the good news, and they were the first to shout the good news. They had seen and heard something wonderful! God had come to earth. God was right there, lying on a bed of straw.

Have you seen the picture or symbol of a shepherd's staff anywhere in the church? *(Here you may hold up the staff you brought in and/or point out the staff on the church paraments or on a pastor's stole.)* It makes sense for a pastor to wear, or at times even carry, a shepherd's staff, because shepherds were the first people to tell the world that Jesus was born.

All of you can be honorary shepherds, too. You have heard the good news. You know what Christmas is all about. You can shout out to the world that Jesus is born—just as loud as those shepherds did two thousand years ago. Let's all be shouting shepherds together, shall we? Let's all shout, "Merry Christmas! Jesus is born!" *(Try it with the children. Afterward you may hand out candy canes for a treat to take home. Show the children how the canes are shaped like shepherd staffs.)*

We shout and sing, Merry Christmas, dear Jesus, because you have come to earth. Help us to spread the good news far and wide that you were born for all of us.

Notes

At Long Last

H ave any of you ever waited a very long time for something? *(Let children answer.)* How long did you have to wait? A week? A month? Maybe even a year? Have any of you waited your whole life for something? *(Children may respond.)*

Simeon was a man who lived a long time ago in Jerusalem, and he waited his whole life—eighty or ninety years—for something very special to happen. He was waiting to meet somebody very important. Do you know who that important person was? *(Someone may volunteer the name.)*

Simeon was waiting to meet Jesus, the Savior of the world. God had let Simeon know that before he died, he would get to see Jesus in person. Simeon waited his whole life for that moment, and finally when he was an old, old man, it happened.

When Jesus was just a baby, his parents brought him into the temple in Jerusalem. They came to thank God for sending them a special son. They came to thank God for sending them the Savior of the world. That same day that Jesus was brought to the temple, Simeon felt that God was telling him to go to the temple. Simeon knew something very special was going to happen. He was even more excited than the way we feel on Christmas morning. Even though Simeon was an old man, he may have run all the way to the temple.

And when he got there, he knew right away who that little baby was. He took that precious baby in his arms and he burst into song. Simeon, without hesitating, without planning what he was going to say, began to sing a beautiful song.

Have you ever felt like bursting into song? Sometimes you just can't help yourself. *(You may ask one who responds what they might sing when they burst into song. If you like, you can give your own impromptu song.)* Mary and Joseph must have been surprised, don't you think? A dignified old man comes up to them, asks to hold their baby, and then bursts into song.

Actually, I think that was a good thing—in fact, just the *right* thing—for Simeon to do. We should burst into song more often when we think about Jesus. God sent us a Savior. God sent Jesus! So if you feel like singing today, you go ahead and sing. God will be listening.

Dear God, we praise you for filling our hearts with songs to sing. We praise you for sending Jesus to us and giving us something wonderful to sing about.

Notes

A Watered Garden

Preparation: Bring a watering can and packets of seeds. You may even bring some potted flowers, seedlings, or seeds to hand out to the children.

I'd like to read one verse from the Bible to you. It's part of the Old Testament reading: Jeremiah, chapter 31, verse 12. "God's people will come home and sing songs on the heights of Jerusalem. They will be radiant because of the many gifts the Lord has given them—the good crops of wheat, wine, and oil, and the healthy flocks and herds. Their life will be like a watered garden, and all their sorrows will be gone" (NLT).

"Their life will be like a watered garden . . ." What a wonderful word picture! What is a watered garden like? What would you find in a watered garden? *(Let children offer their responses.)* You would find green things growing, wouldn't you? Flowers, vegetables, bushes, fruit trees, shade trees—all of these things can grow and thrive in a watered garden.

Let's pretend we've planted a garden here at the front of the church. What sorts of things would you see here? What would you like to find in a garden? *(Listen to answers and offer your own favorites.)* It sounds like we have a wonderful garden here! Now, what would happen to our garden if we all went away and nobody watered or took care of it for a long time? The garden would wither and die, wouldn't it?

We all have something like a garden inside each of us. Our "inside garden" is filled with our thoughts, our discoveries,

and our feelings. Our garden is who we are deep inside. Who do you suppose waters our inside gardens? Who fills us with love and good thoughts and healthy feelings? *(A child may answer.)* Yes, God is our gardener; and if we let him tend the garden, how will the garden grow? Our garden will be very healthy and fruitful. When we pray and listen to God and read our Bibles and obey God, then we stay healthy inside.

I hope that all of your lives will be like a watered garden. Before you go back to your places, let's water our pretend garden and watch the plants sprout up. *(Use your watering can to pretend to water the garden. You or the children may comment on the pretend plants sprouting.)* Thank you for gardening with me this morning.

Dear Lord, our loving gardener, water our lives with your love and keep us free from the weeds and thorns of bad thoughts. Help us to grow up healthy inside and out.

Notes

Turn Around

C an anyone tell me what the word *repent* means? *(Child may offer a definition.)* If you are doing something bad and you repent, what do you do? You stop doing the wrong thing and begin doing the right thing. The word *repent* means "to turn around and go the other way." Could I have a volunteer to help demonstrate the word *repent*? *(Pick a volunteer.)*

I would like our helpful volunteer to walk down the center aisle toward the back of the church until you hear me say, "Repent!" That word is almost the same as "About face!" When you hear "Repent!," you turn around and come back. Let's try it. *(Let the volunteer get partway down the aisle and then call them back with the word* repent.*)* Did this person repent? Yes, they turned around and came back. If only we all could repent as quickly as that!

Before Jesus began preaching, a man named John the Baptist told people to repent. He told them they were going the wrong way; they weren't thinking about God at all. He wanted them to stop walking away from God, to turn around and walk toward God. And when someone had repented, John the Baptist would baptize him or her in the river.

Was this the same kind of baptism that happens here in church on some Sundays? Was this the same kind of baptism that you had when you were a baby? No, not quite. John's baptism and Jesus' baptism were different. John was sent by God to get people ready for Jesus. He turned them around and got them to face the right direction. John baptized with water to show that the people had repented and were now living good, clean lives. When you are baptized in the name of the Father, Son, and Holy Spirit, your sin is washed away and something else happens: you are brought into God's family. In baptism, you become a child of God.

But even though we belong to God and have been baptized into God's family, we sometimes go in the wrong direction. We sometimes turn away from God and do bad things. That's when we need to remember the word *repent*. Then we can turn around and face the right direction. And God will help us repent and turn around.

(After the prayer, you may have all the children practice "doing" the word repent by having them face forward and then turn around to face their parents before returning to their seats. You may say something like the following.) Let's have everyone face me. Now I'm going to ask all of you to repent and turn to face the other direction. You can all turn around and face your families, and go join them once again.

Forgive us, Lord Jesus, when we go the wrong way. Help us to repent, to turn around and walk with you down the right path. Thank you for forgiving us and walking with us.

Notes

Wonderfully Made

Preparation: Bring an ink pad and small squares of smooth, white paper for making children's fingerprints; or you may use your own pre-made thumbprints to hand out. You may also bring magnifying glasses to help the children study their fingerprints.

The Psalm for today is beautiful. Psalm 139, verses 13 and 14 read, "You made all the delicate, inner parts of my body and knit me together in my mother's womb. Thank you for making me so wonderfully complex! Your workmanship is marvelous—and how well I know it" (NLT). God knew us even before we were born. He knows our every detail. He knows us inside and out.

Have you ever thought about what an amazing creation a human being is? There are so many parts to our bodies, and they usually all work together just the way they are designed to work. Our brains send the right signals to control the many functions in our bodies. Our bones support us, our muscles move us, and our skin protects us. We are wonderfully made!

What do you think is the best thing your body can do? Is the best thing being able to taste food with your tongue, or maybe to sing with your voice? *(Let the children talk about what they think is the best.)*

Our sense of touch is an amazing thing. Have any of you felt a fly or a mosquito land on your arm? That's an extremely light touch to be able to feel. Our fingers are especially sensitive. Your fingers can feel the slightest little scratch on a smooth glass surface.

Look at your fingertips. Can you see your fingerprints? A fingerprint is the pattern of tiny bumps and ridges on the tip of your finger. Your fingerprints are unique; no one has the same fingerprints as anyone else. Up close, they are amazing. Some are swirls, some are circles or waves. And God knows every detail of each of us, down to the last fingerprint.

I'd like to give you each something to take home with you to remind you that you are wonderfully made and very special. *(If you have a small number of children, you can let each do a fingerprint. Have someone help with the process, making sure they wipe their hands afterward.)* I brought an ink pad and paper so that we could make fingerprints. *(If you have a large number of children, you could quickly pass out pre-made thumb prints and encourage the kids to do their own prints at home.)*

God made each one of you unique. There is no one in the world just like you. And God loves you for who you are. He knows everything about you down to your fingertips. Let's thank God for doing such a wonderful job in creating you.

Thank you dear Lord, our awesome Creator, for making us in such a wonderful way. Thank you for all of our senses and for making each one of us different and unique.

Notes

Hiding from God

Preparation: Bring a large blanket or dark-colored sheet.

Have any of you heard about a man named Jonah? *(Let children respond.)* Jonah was a prophet of God; he would listen to God and tell the people what God said. One day, God told Jonah to go to a big city and tell the people who lived there that they were being very wicked and that they needed to change their ways. Jonah did not want to do this. He didn't like the people in that city, and maybe he was afraid of them. Jonah decided to run away and hide from God, so he caught the first ship out of town and away he went.

Do you think Jonah was able to hide from God? What if Jonah hid way down deep inside a ship? Could he hide from God there? *(Let children answer.)* Well, Jonah did hide in a ship. But God sent a big storm and tossed that boat around so much that the other sailors thought they were going to drown. They found out that it was Jonah's fault that their ship was being blown about, so do you know what they did? *(Let children respond.)* They tossed him overboard, and the storm stopped.

Did God let Jonah drown? No! What did he send to save Jonah? *(Children may answer.)* A great big fish. And what did the fish do? It swallowed Jonah, and Jonah sat in the belly of the fish. Was it a good hiding place from God? No. God can always see us.

(Here you may offer your own story about hiding. My example follows.) I know a little girl who would tiptoe past me with her hands over her eyes. She figured that if she couldn't see me, I

couldn't see her. Does that work? No. I could still see her. There are people today—even grownups—who think that if they can't see God, that God doesn't exist. Is that true? No. That's like tiptoeing around with your hands over your eyes.

Should we try hiding this morning? Let's all close our eyes and try to hide from the congregation. Everyone close your eyes. *(Now speak to the congregation.)* Can you still see us? That didn't work too well. But I brought a big blanket with me today. I bet if we all get under it, we'll be able to hide. Let's try it! *(All get under blanket.)*

Now the congregation can't see us, can they? But can God still see us? Yes. We can't hide from God. He is always watching over us because he loves us and wants to protect us.

Do you know what finally happened to Jonah? The big fish brought Jonah to shore, and Jonah did finally go to that big city. The people listened to Jonah and stopped doing the bad things. Their lives changed because Jonah finally brought to them the message from God.

Lord God in heaven, we can't hide from you. You know what we do and what we think. Give us the strength and courage to do all the things that you want us to do.

Notes

Love Builds the Church

Preparation: You may bring a hammer and nails or some other construction tools.

The Bible reading from 1 Corinthians today talks about building up the church. If you were going to help build up the church, what sort of tools do you think you might need? *(Discuss.)* I brought some tools with me *(show the tools)*, but the trouble is, I'm not sure I know enough about how to use these tools to build. And I'm not sure I know enough about other things either—about the church, about the people in church, and about God. I may not know enough to build up the church.

I'd like you to raise your hand if you think you know a lot. Raise your hand if you think you have lots of knowledge and could answer lots of questions about the church and about God. *(Let children participate.)* Now who thinks your parents know even more than you do? Raise your hand if you think your parents know more about these things than you do.

Okay, now I have a question to ask you. Do you think it is the people who know the most that can really build up the church? Are they the ones that make the church strong and healthy? *(Let children answer.)* Listen to how the Bible answers that question.

First Corinthians 8:1-3 says, "While knowledge may make us feel important, it is love that really builds up the church. Anyone who claims to know all the answers doesn't really know very much. But the person who loves God is the one God knows and cares for" (NLT). It isn't the people who know a lot that build up the church, is it? What really builds up the church? *(Let children answer.)* Love builds up the church. The church is really the people who make up the family of God. The building isn't as important as the people, is it?

And it turns out that knowing a lot isn't as important as loving a lot. Being smart may make us feel important, but loving others and being helpful with your words and actions is really what makes the church grow strong. Love makes God's family stronger, and love also brings more people into God's family.

It looks like I won't be needing these tools. I think all of you are plenty skilled enough to build up this church. All of you know how to show love for each other, so let's get to work. On your way back to your places this morning, I want you to help build up the church by showing two other people that you care about them. You could give them a smile, a hug, or a handshake, or just tell them that you love them.

Loving God, help make us good workers in your church by teaching us how to build up the family of God with love.

Notes

Soaring Like an Eagle

Preparation (optional): Bring a picture of a soaring eagle to illustrate your sermon.

How many of you have seen an eagle or a hawk soaring high in the sky? *(Let children respond.)* It's amazing to watch, isn't it? The beautiful bird will spread its wings wide and make big circles in the sky. An eagle can make flying look easy. It doesn't have to beat its wings to stay way up in the air.

But, a hummingbird is quite different from an eagle, isn't it? Both are incredibly beautiful birds, but an eagle is very large with huge wings, and a hummingbird is tiny. Can anyone tell me the differences between the way an eagle flies and the way a hummingbird flies? *(Discuss with the children.)* A hummingbird has to beat its wings very fast to get where it wants to go or just to keep itself up in the air. An eagle can beat its wings slowly—or not at all—and still keep flying.

Have you ever felt like an eagle? There's a verse in the book of Isaiah that says people who trust in God are like eagles. Isaiah 40, verse 31 gives a wonderful word picture. Try to see this in your mind as I read the verse. "Those who wait on the Lord will find new strength. They will fly high on wings like eagles. They will run and not grow weary. They will walk and not faint" (NLT).

I have a question for you. Do eagles soar in the sky on their own power? How can they stay way up in the sky for so long without even flapping their wings? *(Someone may offer the correct answer.)* It's not the eagle's own strength that keeps it up in the sky; it is the wind. When the eagle finds a place where warmer air is rising quickly, it can ride that rising column of air higher and higher into the sky, then glide back down to earth. The warm air rising up beneath the wings of the eagle is what keeps the eagle soaring in the sky. *(You may have the children spread their "wings" like eagles and pretend to soar.)*

When we are tired of doing the right thing, tired of being nice, tired of obeying our parents, and are not sure if we can keep doing what we know God wants us to do, where do we get the strength to keep going? *(Children can respond.)* Our strength comes from God, doesn't it? He is like the wind under our wings, helping us to soar like eagles.

If we try to do things on our own, we're more like the little hummingbird, using all our energy just to stay a little way above the ground. We can't do it on our own. But God gives us the strength we need to obey, and he even gives us the faith we need to believe in him. *(After the prayer, you may encourage the children to spread out their "wings" and glide back to their places.)*

Dear Lord, when we are tired or frightened, help us to rely on your strength and let you be the wind beneath our wings.

Notes

In Training

Preparation: Bring or wear a pair of running shoes.

I brought along a pair of running shoes to help remind me to get some exercise today. *(Show your shoes.)* How many of you exercise most days? What do you do for exercise? *(Children may answer.)* Exercise is good for you, isn't it? *(Here you may share an example of a fitness regimen. My example follows.)* I try to exercise at least every other day. I do some jogging, some sit-ups, and some pull-ups. Sometimes if I exercise a lot, I feel really tired.

Let's say I wanted to run in a marathon. That's a very long race, more than twenty miles. A marathon takes hours to run. If the race was tomorrow and I had never run twenty miles in my life, do you think I would win the race? *(Children may respond.)* If I haven't trained for the race, there's not a very good chance of me winning, is there? If I really wanted to win that marathon, what do you suppose I would have to do? *(Let children respond.)* I would have to run almost every day and for a long time. If I trained hard and made that race the most important thing in my life, then I might have a chance at winning.

Did you know that all of you are in a race? You should be training hard. I don't mean that you should be running many miles every day, but you should be practicing listening to God and doing the right thing.

When you are a Christian, the most important thing in your life is following God—and this is like a race, something that takes a lot of effort and strength. Sometimes it's hard to say, "No!" when a friend wants you to do a bad thing. At times, the right thing to do is also the toughest thing to do. But the more you do the right thing, the stronger you become.

The apostle Paul did not have an easy time following Jesus. People threw him in jail and hurt him because he believed in God. It was not easy, but he didn't give up. He was in training, and he was determined to win. First Corinthians is a letter he wrote to encourage other Christians to keep following God's way. He wrote, "Remember that in a race everyone runs, but only one person gets the prize. You also must run in such a way that you will win. All athletes *train hard*. They do it to win a prize that will fade away, but we do it for an eternal prize" (1 Cor. 9:24-25 NLT, author's paraphrase in italics).

At the end of our race, our eternal prize will be that Jesus will be waiting to welcome us into heaven. So the next time you have a tough time doing what God wants you to do, remember that we are all in training, and we need the exercise. Train hard! God has promised to help us get better and better.

Dear Jesus, help us to keep on doing the right thing, even when it's difficult and we want to give up. Make us strong in your love.

Notes

Healing Everything

Preparation: Bring several bottles of medicine, including a bottle of cough syrup.

I f you couldn't get to sleep because you were coughing so much and coughing so hard that your throat was getting sore, what might your mom or dad do to help you? *(Let children respond.)* They might give you cough syrup to calm down the cough so you could sleep. *(Show cough syrup.)* That's what this medicine is used for—to calm coughs. Of course, you would drink this only if a doctor or a parent gave it to you. You have to be very careful with medicine!

I have some other medicines with me. They are all meant to take care of one thing or another: headaches, allergies, upset stomach. I can't find a medicine for one thing, though. What if I had a friend who was lying in bed and couldn't move—someone who was paralyzed? Is there a pill that could make the person get up and walk again? *(Children may respond.)* I have wished many times that there was, but a medicine like that does not exist. Maybe someday, but not yet.

Just like nowadays, there was no medicine for paralyzed people back when Jesus was teaching and healing here on earth. One day when Jesus was preaching in a very crowded house, some men opened a hole in the roof above him. Through that hole, they lowered a paralyzed man until he was lying right in front of Jesus. This man's friends couldn't get through the crowd to take him to Jesus, so they went to the roof and used ropes to lower their friend to Jesus. These friends knew that Jesus was the only one in the world who could heal the man.

Jesus did heal their friend, but do you know what he said first? He said, "My son, your sins are forgiven" (Mark 2:5 NLT). Many people thought that was a strange thing to say and a strange way to heal someone. But what do you think is more important to God—the health of our bodies or the health of our souls? Can you be close to God if your body is healthy but there is hatred and sin in your heart? No! Can you be close to God if your body doesn't work the way it should, but your heart is full of joy and love for Jesus? Yes! Jesus was healing the inside before healing the outside.

Does Jesus always heal our bodies? We may have to wait until we get to heaven before some sicknesses are healed. But will Jesus always forgive us and heal us on the inside? Yes! Always! Jesus forgives our sins and heals our hearts so that we can be close to God. That's the best medicine there is.

Dear Jesus, thank you for healing our hearts. We pray that you would make us healthy on the inside, and we also ask for health and healing for our bodies.

Notes

Who Needs a Doctor?

Preparation: Bring a doctor's bag or kit with items that a doctor might carry.

I brought a doctor's bag with me this morning. It has things in it that a doctor might use. *(Open bag and show items. My examples follow.)* Here's a stethoscope to listen to your heart, an instrument to look into someone's ear, a tongue depressor to check the mouth and throat, and medicine that a doctor might give someone to help them feel better.

When do you go to a doctor? Have any of you gone to the doctor recently? *(Let children respond.)* You usually go to the doctor when you're sick. That's when you really need a doctor to help you.

Jesus is sort of like a doctor. He heals a lot of people. He even brought some people back from the dead. He has great power to heal; but he doesn't heal just a person's body, he also heals their soul. And when Jesus was healing here on earth, he did not just wait for people to come to him. He walked right up to people who were hurting inside, people who really needed help, and he healed their souls.

Jesus walked right up to a man named Levi and told him, "Come, be my disciple" (Mark 2:14 NLT). Levi was a tax collector. He was a liar and a cheater, and nobody in his town wanted anything to do with him. His only friends were other tax collectors. But Levi didn't wait to be asked twice. He knew that Jesus could save his soul. He left his tax-collecting booth and followed Jesus. That same night, Jesus went to

Levi's house for dinner and ate with a bunch of other people who used bad language, did bad things, and didn't ever go to church. They had all come to see and hear Jesus. They wanted to change. The Pharisees, the people who always went to church, were shocked! They said, "Why does Jesus eat with such scum?" Jesus answered them, "Healthy people don't need a doctor—sick people do. I have come to call sinners, not those who think they are already good enough" (Mark 2:16–17 NLT). The Pharisees didn't think they needed Jesus, but the Bible says that everyone has sinned. We all need Jesus' forgiveness.

When we tell other people about Jesus or when we invite someone to church who has never been to church before, we have to remember that we need Jesus just as much as they do. Because we know how good it feels to be healed by Jesus, we can feel good about bringing others to him, too. We can share Bible stories and tell friends how Jesus has healed our hearts and forgiven our sins. And then we can be healers like Jesus.

Jesus, we bring our hurting hearts and lives to you for healing. Help us to tell others, as one sinner to another, that you are the source of healing for all.

Notes

The Real Jesus

Preparation: Bring a scarf that can completely cover your head and shoulders. You should be able to see out, but others won't clearly see your face. Begin the children's time with the scarf already on your head.

How many of you know who I am? Raise your hand if you know who I am. *(Let a child tell your name.)* Good. You all know who I am even if I have this scarf covering my face and head. But how can you tell it's me if you can't see my face? *(Children will respond.)* You can recognize my voice, you can see how tall and how big I am, you can see the clothes I'm wearing, and you can tell how I act. Even if my face is covered, you can still tell who I am.

What if the only way you had ever seen me was with a scarf over my head and face? What if I walked around like this all the time? You could still get to know me. We could talk and do things together even if you couldn't see my face. I can see through this scarf fairly well. I can see all of you, but you can't see me very well.

If I take the scarf off, you can see who I am much more clearly. *(At this point, remove the scarf from your face.)*

Today is Transfiguration Sunday. The word *transfiguration* means a change in looks or appearance. We read in the Bible how Jesus took three of his close friends up to the top of a mountain with him. While they were up there, something amazing happened. Before their very eyes, Jesus changed. It

was as if a light began to shine brightly inside Jesus. His face and body, and even his clothes, began to shine brightly. And then two prophets from long ago suddenly appeared near Jesus and began speaking with him.

This transfiguration was as if a scarf had been pulled away from the face of Jesus and suddenly the disciples could see Jesus for who he really was. Jesus was a true man; he was a person like his friends. But he was also God. For this glorious moment, the disciples were able to see Jesus as true man and true God.

Sometimes in our own lives, scarves are pulled away. As we get to know people, we begin to see them more clearly. When you're little, you see your mom and dad as people who take care of you. They clothe you, feed you, and love you. As you get older, you see something new about your parents—that they need love, too. They need help from you and from others. You begin to see them more clearly, and so you are able to know them better and love them better.

Dear Lord Jesus, help us to see others more clearly. And help us especially to see you more clearly. And as we see you, help us to be like you.

Notes

Sitting on the Rainbow

Preparation: Bring a picture of a rainbow or of Noah's ark with the rainbow above it. You may also bring candy in rainbow colors to hand out at the end of the sermon.

R aise your hands if you've ever seen a rainbow. Can you tell me what a rainbow looks like? *(Choose a volunteer to describe a rainbow.)* Rainbows are beautiful, aren't they? What is the shape of a rainbow? *(Let a child answer.)*

We usually see a rainbow as an arc in the sky. Sometimes we might even see a half-circle stretching from the land, up into the sky, then back down to the land. *(Describe the shape with your gestures as you talk.)* But did you know that a rainbow is actually a circle? Usually, we can't see the whole circle from where we're standing. Clouds or buildings may get in the way, or there may not be enough moisture in the air to catch the light, and then you can't see the whole rainbow.

If there is enough mist in the air and the sun hits the mist just right, you might be able to see an entire rainbow circle. You can create your own rainbow if you go outside on a sunny day with a hose and spray a fine mist into the air. Then watch the mist carefully; you should be able to see a rainbow form. And if you're sitting just right, you will see a rainbow that starts on one side of you, goes up into the air, and comes down to end on the other side of you. You will be sitting in the middle of a rainbow!

(Here you may offer your own rainbow story. My example follows.) One day I saw an entire rainbow—the whole circle! I

had hiked to the bottom of a huge waterfall. I thanked God for such an awesome, beautiful place. Suddenly, something incredible happened—a brilliant rainbow started to form. On my right side, the bright colors began. The rainbow circled up into the waterfall then around back to me and ended at my left side. I could put my hand through the rainbow. I was sitting on a rainbow!

The rainbow is a beautiful reminder that God made a promise to Noah and all the creatures of the earth after the great flood. God promised that he loves all his creatures, and he would never again cover the world with water. This was a promise to Noah, but it is also a promise to us. God loves us very much, too, and he wants to be first in our lives.

We are a part of God's rainbow promise. The rainbow promise is a circle. It begins with God, comes to us, and goes back up to God. You are sitting on the rainbow—in the middle of God's promise.

Thank you, dear God, for sending the rainbow as a promise of love to us. Help us always to remember that each one of us is sitting on that rainbow.

Notes

Get Behind Me

Preparation: You may bring along a photo of one of your best friends and be ready to tell the children about your friend.

Raise your hand if you have a really good friend—a best friend—that you like to play with. Can you tell me about one of your friends? What do you like about that friend? (*Let several children describe one of their friends.*)

I have some good friends, too. (*Here you may show the children a photo of your friend and tell them what you like about the friend. My example follows.*) My best friend is my husband, Joel. One of the reasons I enjoy his company so much is that we can play silly games together. We used to play a game where we'd run around and try to catch leaves that were falling to the ground in our teeth. It's a very difficult thing to do because leaves flutter this way and that way as they fall. It makes you laugh trying to do it, and it is very funny to watch! It's fun to play silly games with friends.

Did you know that Jesus had close friends, too? The Bible talks about one of Jesus' closest friends, Peter. Jesus called Peter a "rock." Peter was a good friend; he was someone you could count on. Do you have a friend like that?

What would you do if your friend tried to get you to do something that was bad? How would you answer them if they told you to hit or tease someone? What if they wanted you to take something that wasn't yours? If that happened to you, what should you tell your friend? (*Let children answer.*)

We like our friends, and we want them to like us, but if they

want us to do the wrong thing, we need to tell them that we can't go along with them. If they are *true* friends, they will remain your friends even when you say "No" to their bad ideas.

Peter once tried to get Jesus to do the wrong thing. Jesus told his disciples that he would have to die on the cross. That was what he came to earth to do. God sent Jesus to save us from our sins. But Peter did not want this to happen. He told Jesus not to go to the cross. Do you know how Jesus answered Peter? *(Someone may offer the correct answer.)*

To Peter, his very good friend, Jesus said, "Get behind me, Satan!" (Mark 8:33 NRSV). Satan is another name for the devil. Would the devil want Jesus to save the world from sin? No, he wouldn't. Satan would try to stop Jesus, even if he had to use one of Jesus' friends to do so. Jesus was showing Peter that it was wrong to try to stop him from dying on the cross. Maybe Peter's feelings were hurt, but he didn't stop being Jesus' friend. He knew that Jesus had to do the right thing.

Dear Jesus, thank you for blessing us with good friends. Help us all to encourage each other to do the right thing—the thing that would please you. And if our friends want us to do bad things, make us strong to tell them "No."

Notes

Holy Name

D oes everyone here have a name? Names are important aren't they? Everybody has a name. Let's hear some of your names. *(Let children respond.)* How do you feel about your name? Do you like it? *(Children may share.)* You should feel good about your name. It is very precious. When you were just a tiny baby, you received your name. The best name for you that could be thought of was picked.

What names does God have? Tell me all the names you can remember. *(Responses may vary.)* Lord, Father in heaven, Jesus, Christ, Holy Spirit; those are all names that refer to the one God whom we worship. God's name is very special, too, isn't it?

How would you feel if someone wrote your name on a piece of paper, held it up for everyone to see, and then stepped on it? That wouldn't feel very good, would it? Has anyone ever teased you about your name or used your name to say something mean? That's not a nice thing to do, is it? You wouldn't want someone to misuse your name and step on it or say something mean about it. It would be just like they were being mean to you.

Have you ever heard someone using God's name in bad ways? In the middle of a conversation, you might hear someone say something like, "Oh, God! I was so embarrassed!" Or if someone is angry, they might say, "Jesus! That hammer hit me right on the thumb!" Are those people really thinking about God when they use his name that way? No. It's like stepping on the name of the Lord. When someone uses God's name in that way they are not honoring God's name; instead, they are being careless with it.

God gave us Ten Commandments, and the Third Commandment is a very important one. It says, "You shall not take the name of the Lord your God in vain" (Exod. 20:7 RSV). Another translation reads, "Do not misuse the name of the Lord your God" (NLT). Using God's name without thinking about God, or using his name to say something bad, is misusing God's name. This is something that displeases God.

It's sad when people misuse God's name. It's just the same as being mean to God. But you'll probably hear people doing just that. Sometimes even Christians forget and misuse God's name. You won't be able to stop everyone from stepping on God's name. But if, for example, you have friends over to play, and you hear them using God's name carelessly in your house, you can politely ask them to stop. You can tell them that in your house, God's name is special.

Help us to honor your name always, Lord God, in all of the words that we speak. Keep us from using your name in a careless way.

Notes

Look Up

Preparation: Bring a cross to hold up so that the children can look up to it.

How many of you can remember a time when you felt very sick? *(Children can raise their hands or respond.)* Have you ever felt so sick and weak that you couldn't get out of bed? Or so sick that you could hardly move at all?

When Moses was in the desert with the Israelites, there was a time when lots of people got bitten by snakes and became very sick. They were so sick they couldn't move, and they almost died. God told Moses to make a statue of a snake mounted on a tall pole and to show it to the sick people. The people needed only to look up at that snake and they would get better right away.

This morning, I'd like for us to try something. We're going to pretend that we're so weak and sick that we can't get up. You can lie down if you want to or just sit right where you are. Just make sure that you can still see me from where you are.

We'll pretend that we're so sick that we can't move our toes, our feet, or our legs. We are so weak we can't move our hips, and our stomach muscles don't work anymore. It's getting worse now, because we can't move our fingers, our hands, or our arms. I'm not going to be as sick as all of you, because I have to keep talking; but I want you to pretend that you are so sick now, that you can't even move your head.

Keep your eyes open, though, because I want you to look at me. Even though you can't move your body or your head,

Sitting on the Rainbow

you can still look at me, can't you? You can look up. *(Hold a cross up so everyone can see it.)* Can everyone see this cross? All you have to move is your eyes, and you can see the cross.

When we sin and do things we know we should not, it is like being sick. We're sick in our hearts, and we need to be made better. When Jesus died on the cross, he was raised up like that snake on a pole that Moses made. And, like the Israelites in the desert, everyone who looks up to Jesus on the cross and believes in him, will not die. They will be saved and have eternal life.

Do we have to jump up high or climb up to God in heaven for God to save us? No. We are not saved by anything we can do. Jesus saved us when he died on the cross. We only have to look up to him and believe in him.

Do you know the Bible verse, John 3:16? Let's say it together: "For God so loved the world that he gave his only Son, that whoever believes in him should not perish, but have eternal life" (RSV).

Jesus, we cannot be saved or even come to believe in you by any effort of our own. We look to you to save us from sin and to bring us everlasting life.

Notes

Coming Clean

Preparation: Bring a small bottle of vegetable or olive oil, a damp cloth, and soap.

Have you ever gotten oil on your hands and then tried to wash it off with water? Does the oil rinse off? *(Let children respond.)* No, it doesn't come off with just water, does it? What else do you need to get oil off your hands? *(Someone may offer the correct answer.)* Right: you need soap.

Psalm 51 talks about getting clean. King David wrote this psalm after he had done something very wrong. He was sorry for what he did, and he asked God to forgive him and make him clean again. King David wrote, "Wash me thoroughly and cleanse me from my sin. Wash me and I shall be whiter than snow" (v. 7 author's paraphrase).

King David didn't really need soap to get himself clean. He needed forgiveness from God. Forgiveness is a little bit like soap, though. When we sin, we may try to cover the sin up, to ignore the "dirt" or to hide it from others. We may tell ourselves, "Well, it's not so bad what I did; other people have done it, too." That's like trying to wash dirty oil off our hands with water; it doesn't work.

Just as we need soap to get oil off our hands, we need Jesus' forgiveness to come clean from our sins. God wants us to admit that we've done wrong. This is called confession. And when we confess to God that we've done something wrong, God forgives us and makes us clean inside.

I brought oil with me this morning, so let's experiment with it. I'll rub oil over my hands and then I'll try rinsing it off in this bowl of water. *(Do this now.)* I'll let some of you feel my hands. *(Let those nearest you check your oil.)* Did the oil come off? It didn't, did it? You can't really see the oil, but it's still there. And sometimes other people may not know about our sins or see our sins, but God knows—God knows us completely. He knows we need forgiveness. The sin sticks to us sort of like the oil sticks to my hands.

Now let's try soap. *(Wash with soap and water; dry your hands. Then have kids check again.)* Are my hands finally clean? Yes, now they're clean, but I needed the soap to get clean, didn't I? We also need God's forgiveness to make us truly clean inside.

The next time you need to get really clean—clean inside—remember that only God's forgiveness can wash away our sin. And remember that God is happy to forgive us because he loves us.

We're sorry, dear Jesus, for the times when we do the wrong thing. Thank you for forgiving us and making us clean inside.

Notes

The Pain of Separation

Preparation: Arrange for a mother and infant to be present, or invite a parent to accompany his or her child to the front.

What do you suppose would happen if a little baby was snuggled in close to her mommy, having some nice warm milk, and suddenly someone took that baby away from her mother? How would the baby react? *(Let children respond.)* The baby would cry, wouldn't she? And the mommy would probably be upset, too. Babies need their mommies and daddies to love and protect them, to feed them, and keep them clean and dry. Being away from loving parents can make a baby very sad, especially if the baby is hungry. And when you hear a baby crying for its mommy or daddy, it's a sad thing.

Jesus had to do something very sad, too. Today is Palm Sunday. It's the day we remember the story of Jesus riding a donkey into Jerusalem while the crowds cheered and laid palm branches in his path. But the joy of Palm Sunday has a dark shadow following it. Palm Sunday is the beginning of Holy Week, when we remember Jesus' suffering and death. If we go right from the joy of Palm Sunday to the celebration of Easter, we've missed something very important.

As Jesus rode into Jerusalem, he knew that he was going to die on the cross, be buried in a tomb, and after three days, come back to life again. For a short time, Jesus was going to be separated from his friends and family on earth. Do you think that made Jesus sad? How do you think it made his close friends feel? *(Let children answer.)*

Before Jesus came back to life, he would be separated from people he loved very much—people who loved him and needed him to be with them. And that kind of separation is a sad thing.

We need Jesus, and Jesus wants to be near us in the same way that babies and parents need and want each other. But Jesus was not gone from them for long. After three days, he came back to be with them again—and to be with them forever and ever. Because Jesus died and came back to life, he made sure that all of us would never ever have to be separated from him. We know that even when we die, Jesus will be with us and give us a new and better life—just like the new life he has.

We never need to feel like we're away from Jesus and our heavenly Father. The next time you're snuggled up in the arms of someone you love, remember that God is always near, and he will always be near. He's as close as your heart.

Hold us close, Lord. We want to be near you always. Thank you for going to Jerusalem to face death on the cross so that we could be close to God forever.

Notes

Easter Butterflies

Preparation: Bring a picture of a caterpillar, a chrysalis, and a butterfly—or, if possible, bring a real chrysalis and butterfly model.

Happy Easter! The Lord is risen. Hallelujah! Today we celebrate one of the most important days in the church. We celebrate because Jesus rose up from the dead, because he came back to life and is living even today. Many times we have heard the story of how Jesus died on the cross and then beat death by coming back to life on the third day. Easter is not a surprise for us, but it is a wonderful celebration.

The followers of Jesus were surprised on that first Easter. They were shocked. They didn't know what to think. Even though Jesus had told them he would die and then be raised again to life, they just couldn't believe it.

Early on that first Easter morning, three women followers of Jesus went to the tomb where Jesus had been buried. The tomb was a cave dug into the side of a hill where the body of Jesus had been wrapped up with linen cloths and placed on a bench of stone.

The women had many surprises waiting for them that Easter morning. First of all, they were surprised to see that the huge stone had been rolled away from the doorway— the tomb was open. Then they bent down and went into the burial cave and were startled to see an angel sitting in the tomb. They were surprised again to hear the angel tell them that Jesus was not there; he was alive and already on his way to another town. Then the women turned around and were amazed to see the cloths that had wrapped Jesus were folded and on the stone bench where his body had been.

They ran from the tomb, too scared to say anything. Of course, Jesus had told them that he would die and then be raised to life again, but when it actually happened, it was too surprising for the women to accept at first.

Imagine you had a pet caterpillar, and you watched the caterpillar spin a chrysalis, and then nothing happened for days. *(Here you may show your illustration.)* If you didn't know that butterflies come out of chrysalises, you might think your pet had died. You'd be sad that you had lost your fuzzy caterpillar. But one day, you would see that the chrysalis was empty and a beautiful butterfly was fluttering around.

Butterflies are often used as a symbol of Easter. Butterflies decorate churches at Eastertime to remind us of Jesus' death and resurrection. Like a butterfly coming out of a dead-looking chrysalis, Jesus came out alive from the tomb with a resurrected body that would never die. Happy Easter!

Alleluia! We praise you, mighty Lord, for rising up from the dead to new life. Thank you, Jesus, that we, too, will not die, but will live with you forever in heaven. We praise you for Easter.

Notes

Sharing It All

Preparation: You may bring a brown lunch bag containing a treat or stickers to share with the children at the end of your message.

I f you were sitting down to lunch at school and you saw that the person sitting next to you didn't have anything to eat, what might you do? *(Let children respond.)* You could share your food, couldn't you? It's good to share.

I'm sure that everyone here has at one time or another shared with someone else. And we've each received something that someone else has shared with us. *(You may offer your own story of sharing or receiving here. My example follows.)*

A man who was almost bald visited the family of a good friend. He had just a little fringe of hair around the back of his head. The youngest daughter in the family had lots of thick hair that hung down past her waist. "What beautiful hair!" commented the nearly bald man. He then added, with a smile, "You have so much hair, and I have so little . . . couldn't you give me just a little bit of that hair?" The man, of course, was joking and thought the girl knew that he was joking. But the little girl took his request to heart. "It really isn't fair," she thought, "that I have so much hair, and he has so little." So the girl found some scissors and cut off a nice chunk of her hair. Then, beaming with pleasure, she brought her gift down to the guest.

The man did not mean for the girl to cut her hair and share it with him. But she did this; she shared her hair with someone who needed hair. Some people are very good at

sharing. I've watched kids share their toys, clothes, food, and many other things. So many of you are good at sharing smiles and kind words and even hugs.

One of the Bible readings for today talks about sharing. The believers in the early church shared everything they had. Acts 4 says, "All the believers were of one heart and mind, and they felt that what they owned was not their own; they shared everything they had. . . . There was no poverty among them, because people who owned land or houses sold them and brought the money to the apostles to give to others in need" (vv. 32, 34-35 NLT).

The early believers were so good at sharing what they had that there wasn't a needy person among them. Because everybody shared, everyone had what was needed. If we ask, God will help us also become experts at sharing. And, like many things we do, the more we practice sharing, the better we become at it. So remember to practice sharing this week and see how good you become at it. Don't forget to ask God to help you!

Teach us to be generous with all the gifts that you have given us, Lord. Help make us experts at sharing with others.

Notes

The Author of Life

Preparation: Bring several books by your favorite authors to show the children. Authors who have written children's books will be easier for children to relate to.

Does everyone know what an author is? *(Let children answer.)* An author is someone who has written a book. Do you have any favorite authors? *(Let children share some of their favorites.)* There are many good authors who have written books that we enjoy. A man named A. A. Milne wrote the Winnie the Pooh books. A woman named Astrid Lindgren wrote the Pippi Longstocking books. Margaret Wise Brown wrote *Goodnight Moon* and many other books for children.

(Here you may share with the children some of your favorite authors and the books they wrote. My example follows.) One of my favorite authors is a man named C. S. Lewis. He wrote many books for both grownups and children. When I was in third grade, I started reading his stories about a land called Narnia, and I loved them. The stories were enchanting; they carried you into a magical land where you got to meet many wonderful and wise characters. When I was finished with the books about Narnia, I felt that I had gone on a great adventure.

The New Testament book of Acts, chapter 3, tells of when Jesus' friend Peter talked about a very important author. He talked about the "Author of life." Who do you suppose is the "Author of life"? Peter told his listeners, "You killed the Author of life; but God raised him to life." (v. 15 NLT). Who

is Peter talking about? *(Let children answer.)* The Author of life is Jesus! The world and everything in it was created through Jesus. Isn't it strange that the Author—the creator—of life itself, had that life taken from him?

We are people whom God created. We are like the books that an author writes—books that God writes. Author's books are not only a pleasure and a gift to those who read them, they also show the readers a lot about the author who wrote them. God created us in his own image. We are a little bit like God.

Each one of you will live a life that tells a story. And every day you add more pages to your story. Because you are a child of God, you want your life book to be filled with stories of how you followed God's plan. The story of your life might be filled with adventure; there may be some sad parts, there may be some scary parts. But because you are a child of God, most of your life book should be about love. And at the end of your story, you know that you'll be in heaven with Jesus. That is the best ending to any life story.

Lord Jesus, you are the Author of life. Thank you for giving us life. Help us all to live our lives to your glory.

Notes

Show Your Love

Preparation: Bring a large, brightly colored valentine and a warm jacket to help illustrate your talk.

I f you wanted someone to know you loved him or her, what would you say? *(Let children respond.)* You could simply say, "I love you." Then they would know. Or you could write "I love you" on a piece of paper. Even though Valentine's Day is past, I brought a valentine with me, because sending a valentine is another way to tell someone, "I love you."

What if you couldn't speak and you couldn't write? Would you still be able to let people know that you loved them? *(Let children respond.)* There are lots of other ways to tell people you love them. You could give them a hug or a kiss. You could smile at them or maybe even hold their hand.

It's easy for most of us to show love to members of our family or to friends; but God wants us to love all his children, even those who aren't family or close friends. This doesn't mean that you need to hug everyone you meet—although I'm sure that would make the world a happier place. But it does mean that God wants us to be ready to help others that might be in real need.

1 John 3, verses 17 and 18 read, "But if anyone who has money enough to live well, and sees a brother or sister in need and refuses to help—how can God's love be in that person? Dear children, let us stop just saying we love each other; let us really show it by our actions" (NLT). When John says,

"Dear children," he's talking to grownups, too, because we are, all of us, children of God.

So if you saw a man shivering in the cold outside, and you wanted to show that person you loved him, which of these two things would you give him? *(Hold up both the valentine and the jacket.)* Would you give that cold man a valentine with "I love you" written on it, or would you give him a warm jacket? *(Let the children answer.)* The gift of a warm jacket would be a better way to show your love to that man, wouldn't it?

Of course, you don't have to wait until you see someone shivering in the street to show your love. You can give offering money to help feed people who don't have enough to eat or to help buy Bibles for those who wouldn't get one otherwise. You can show your love for your parents by helping them and doing chores without complaining. When you get home, you and your parents can talk about ways to show love to others by helping them.

Little children, let us show our love by our actions.

Dear God of love, help us tell others that we love them by using both our words and our actions. Thank you for showing your love for us by sending your Son, Jesus.

Notes

No Fear

C an you think of a time when you were really afraid? What was it that made you scared? *(Let children share.)* When did you stop being scared? What was it that comforted you or made you stop being afraid? *(Children can tell about their experiences.)* When we are scared, it can make all the difference in the world to have someone who loves us close by. Knowing that someone loves us and is there to protect and comfort us can make our fear disappear.

(You may discuss fearful times the children might have experienced, or you may share a time when you felt afraid and then comforted. My example follows.) When my mother was a little girl, she lived on a farm in northern Minnesota. She had to walk to and from school, which was about a mile away. One day, in the middle of winter, a blizzard blew in from the north. When school let out and they started home, it was snowing heavily and the wind was blowing very hard right in their faces. They knew they would have to walk all the way across a frozen lake to reach home. My mother was afraid they wouldn't make it, that they might get lost in the snow and never reach home. Suddenly, all her fears disappeared. There, right in front of them, stood her father with a toboggan ready to pull them home. He tucked my mother, her brother, and her sister into the sled and covered them up with a big buffalo-skin robe. Then he pulled them all the way home.

There are many things in our world that might make us feel afraid. But do you ever feel afraid of God? *(Talk about the responses to this question.)* Do you think that God wants us to be afraid of him? The Bible tells us that God is love and that there is no fear in love. 1 John, chapter 4, says that if we really understand God's love for us and let ourselves be wrapped up in that love, then we will have no fear.

God does not want us to be afraid of him. He wants us to know that he loves us so much that we need to have no fear at all. God is love, and when his love fills us, there is no room left for fear.

God does not want us to be afraid of other things in this world either. Of course, we should stay away from dangerous things so that we don't get hurt. You shouldn't ever touch a gun or take drugs that your parents or doctor haven't given to you. But being careful is much different from being afraid. God wants us to live our lives without fear. God has promised to be with us always; nothing in the whole world can take God's love away from us. The next time that you start to feel afraid, remember that God is there, God's love is surrounding you, and there is no need to be afraid.

Surround us with your perfect love, dear God, and help us to live our lives with no fear. Thank you for wrapping us up in your love.

Notes

Love My Kids

Preparation (optional): Arrange for several older members of the congregation to bring small photos of their grandkids and be prepared to show them to the kids during the children's time.

How many of you have grandparents? Raise your hand. I know quite a few grandparents, and all of them just love their grandkids. They love to have their grandchildren visit them, and they tell their friends how wonderful and sweet their grandchildren are. Most grandparents carry around pictures of their grandkids in their wallets and their purses.

Are there any grandparents here this morning who would be willing to show us pictures of their grandchildren? *(Your prearranged grandparents may come up to show the kids their pictures and say just a few words about the grandchildren.)*

I'd like to know how each of you got your grandparents to love you so much. Did you pay them lots of money? Do you take them out to fancy restaurants every week? Are you always extra good when they're around—never complaining about anything, never fighting with your brother or sister? *(Listen to responses.)*

Your grandparents love you for who you are, don't they? Your mom or dad is their child. They love your parents, and they love you. In 1 John, chapter 5, the Bible says, "Every one who believes that Jesus is the Christ is a child of God, and everyone who loves the parent loves the child" (v. 1 RSV).

Who are the children of God? *(A child may give the correct answer.)* All who believe in Jesus are children of God. Our heavenly Father is the parent, and his children are sitting all around you. Some of God's children are young, like you, and some are older like your parents and grandparents. We are all children of God.

The Bible says that everyone who loves the parent also loves the child. Just like your grandparents love the parent (your mom or dad) and love the child (you), so, too, all of us who love God, the heavenly parent, should love all of God's children.

If God had pictures of all of his children in his wallet, how big do you suppose that wallet would have to be? Really big! God has many children. We're part of a big family, aren't we? We're a family of believers, and God wants us to love everybody else in our family.

Dear God, help us love all of your children as much as you do.

Notes

Like a Tree

Preparation (optional): You may bring a couple of small, leafy branches for your young volunteers to hold while they pretend to be trees.

Trees are nice, aren't they? I really like trees, and I think God must like them, too. He made so many of them, and so many different kinds! I'd like to read to you verses from the very first psalm in the Bible—Psalm 1, verses 1 through 3—because it talks about trees.

"Oh the joys of those who do not follow the advice of the wicked . . . but they delight in doing everything the Lord wants; day and night they think about his law. They are like trees planted along the riverbank, bearing fruit each season without fail. Their leaves never wither, and in all they do, they prosper" (NLT).

These verses tell us that a follower of God is like a tree. If we had some trees here to talk with, we might be able to understand this a little better. Could I have a couple of volunteers to be trees this morning? *(Pick two volunteers to interview.)* I'd like our trees to stand up tall with their branches outstretched, and be ready to answer a few questions. *(Have two kids get into place. You may hand them small branches to hold.)*

(Interview both trees, asking what is most important to them or what it is they need to survive. My example follows.) Hello! You're a fine looking tree. I'd like to know: what is the most important thing to you? *(Let "tree" answer, but guide the*

answer to include the sun.) The sun is pretty important to a tree, isn't it? Of course, trees need other things as well, like water and minerals and clean air. But without the sun, there can be no life at all. Did you know that the "Son" also is important to the life of a Christian? This time, though, I'm talking about the Son of God, Jesus. Just as a tree needs the sun to grow and be strong, we need God's Son to grow as Christians and be strong in the Lord. *(Thank the trees and invite them to sit down with you again.)*

I'd like you to say a verse with me from 1 John 5:12. It's a good verse to memorize. "He who has the Son has life" (RSV). *(Have kids repeat the verse a couple of times.)* Today, when you see a beautiful tree with its new leaves stretching toward the sun, remember this verse. "He who has the Son has life."

We thank you, Lord, for sending your Son, Jesus, who brings us everlasting life.

Notes

Spirit of Creation

Preparation: Bring puzzle pieces to give out at the end of the talk.

T oday is Pentecost Sunday. Do you know what happened on the first Pentecost? *(Children may offer answers.)* After Jesus had gone back up to heaven, his disciples were gathered together in a room. Suddenly, there was a sound of rushing wind. It was a mighty sound, and it filled the room. Fire appeared above the heads of each of the disciples, and they began to speak in many different languages.

At Pentecost, the disciples were filled with God's Holy Spirit. It's hard to picture in our minds what the Holy Spirit is like. We can picture Jesus as he might have looked wearing a long robe just like other men did at that time. We may even be able to imagine what God the Father might look like seated on a throne in heaven. But it's hard to get an image in our mind of what the Holy Spirit might be like.

At Pentecost, God's Holy Spirit came as the sound of a rushing wind. The Spirit of God also is mentioned many times in the Old Testament. Verses 25 and 30 of Psalm 104 tell us that this Spirit is creative and life-giving. I'll read a few verses of this psalm to you: "Here is the ocean, vast and wide, teeming with life of every kind, both great and small. . . . When you send your Spirit, new life is born to replenish all the living of the earth" (NLT).

Have we discovered all the creatures in the sea that God's Spirit created? Do you know that scientists who study the oceans are still finding creatures no one has ever seen before?

Sitting on the Rainbow

The Spirit of Pentecost is a great creative force that gives life and faith to us. When we are filled with God's Holy Spirit, we become creative, too.

I have one piece of a puzzle with me today. You can't tell from just this one piece what the whole puzzle looks like, can you? We can know a little bit of what it looks like, though. When you paint a picture, make up a song, play an instrument, or dance and sing to the glory of God, you are seeing a little bit of God's Spirit. God made us to be creative and imaginative because God is creative and imaginative. As you discover the many wonderful things that God's Spirit has created and breathed life into, you see parts of the Holy Spirit. It's sort of like discovering pieces of a puzzle.

The more of God's creation that we discover, the more we are able to see the wonderful creative power of the Holy Spirit. I encourage all of you to keep looking for pieces of the creation puzzle. Use the imagination that God has given you and keep exploring and learning. Before you go back to your seats, take a puzzle piece with you to remind you of God's creative Spirit.

We praise you, Creator and Holy Spirit, for the gift of imagination. Help us use this gift to your glory.

Notes

Abba, Daddy

Preparation: Bring a little bag of treasures or treats to hand out at the end of your message, or you may have the gifts in your pockets.

Imagine that you are visiting at the home of a friend. Your friend's father has been gone on a long trip, and the rest of the family is looking forward to his return. They tell you he'll be coming home soon, and they can't wait to see him again. He's a wonderful father who loves his children very much. Whenever he returns from a trip, his pockets and suitcases are full of wonderful gifts for his children.

Suddenly the front door opens, and there he is. And, sure enough, his pockets are bulging with goodies. Your friend gives a happy shout. "Daddy! Daddy!" she yells and then launches herself in his direction. She lands right in his arms and gets a big bear hug. Her brothers and sisters pile on top of their daddy, too, and hugs and kisses are exchanged all around. Then you watch as he starts to pull from his pockets the marvelous treasures that he has brought home with him.

You are watching all of this from a distance. He's not your daddy, so you're not about to jump into his arms. And even though the pocket treasures look interesting, you are too polite to ask for something yourself. It's an uncomfortable feeling to be left out of a family hug. At this point, you might feel like heading home so that this family can enjoy their time together.

Now imagine that the smiling father who has just returned from a long trip with his pockets full of treasures is

not your friend's father, and not even your own father, but your heavenly Father. What do you think you would do if your heavenly Father stepped through your front door? Would you hang back, too shy to say anything? Would you yell "Daddy" and jump into his arms? *(Let children share their responses.)*

Do you know what God would want you to do? The Bible tells us in Romans, chapter 8, that we should not be shy in front of God, but act like God's own children. We are God's family, and he even expects us to call him "Daddy!" *(The word* Abba *in the original language of this verse is a word that means "Daddy" or "Papa.")*

We really are God's children. We have every right to call our heavenly Father "Daddy" and to leap joyfully into his arms. And the Bible says that, as God's children, we will share in all the riches of his kingdom. Our heavenly Daddy's pockets are filled with love, everlasting life, comfort, peace, and riches that we can't even imagine. *(Before the children return to their seats, share with them some of the "riches" in your pockets.)*

Thank you, God, for being our heavenly Daddy and for adopting us as your own children. Thank you that your arms are always open to us.

Notes

The Company Jesus Keeps

Preparation: Bring a high school or college yearbook, preferably one of your own with pictures of yourself and your classmates.

Have you ever heard the expression, "You are known by the company you keep"? That means if someone looks at your friends, they will know a lot about you. Do you choose friends who are like you? Maybe your friends enjoy playing soccer like you do, or they like the same books you do. Can anyone tell me how you and your friends are alike? *(Let a child talk about his or her friends.)*

I brought along my high-school yearbook so I could show you some friends I had when I was younger. *(Here you may open your yearbook and talk about some of your friends. My example follows.)* It makes me happy to see the faces of these people again because I remember that they were good friends, and we enjoyed being together. Gail, Jaci, and Susan were some friends I grew up with. I've known them since I was in grade school. We liked a lot of the same things. We went biking and swimming together. We liked to have sleep-over parties and stay up late giggling. Do some of you like to do those things, too? *(Allow children to comment.)*

The expression "You are known by the company you keep" usually means we are like the people we hang around with. But there was one time when it didn't mean that. The Gospel of Mark tells about some of the people that Jesus hung around with, and those people were not at all like him. Jesus asked a tax collector named Levi to be his disciple, and Levi dropped what he was doing and followed Jesus. In those days, tax collectors were despised and hated because they often cheated people and took more money than they should.

Nobody in Levi's town would keep company with him. But Jesus was different. He not only talked to the tax collectors and sinners, he even had supper with them. This made the law-abiding, churchgoing leaders of the community angry with Jesus. They asked Jesus' disciples why Jesus ate with sinners and tax collectors. "Why does he eat with such scum?" they asked (Mark 2:16 NLT).

Jesus knew what those people were thinking. He knew they did not love the tax collectors and sinners. But Jesus loved them. Even though he was not like them, Jesus wanted to help them and to save them from their sins. Jesus kept company with people the world hated because he cared about them. This is good news for us because all of us are sinners. We all need Jesus. Praise God that Jesus keeps company with sinners because that means that Jesus keeps company with us.

Dear Jesus, thank you for saving us. Help us carry your love to other sinners who need you just as much as we do.

Notes

Bending the Rules

Preparation: A rulebook of some kind would be a helpful illustration for this sermon, especially a book of traffic rules.

Everyone knows what rules are. Everyone has to follow rules—grown-ups and kids alike. What are some rules that you follow? *(Let children respond.)*

When I was growing up, we had rules in our family, too. These rules were usually followed, but once in a while we had to bend the rules a bit. *(Here you may offer your own story of bending the rules. My example follows.)* One of the rules in my house was, "No eating in your bedroom." This was because it was easier to clean up food messes in the kitchen. If you spilled something in your bedroom, it was a lot of work to clean it up. But, if you were sick in bed, and you didn't feel well enough to get up, you could have your meals in bed. The rule of not eating in the bedroom was bent because a person's health was more important than the rule.

Traffic rules that tell people how to drive safely must be followed by everyone on the road so we don't have accidents. *(You may show your rule book here, giving some examples.)* But even these rules sometimes have to bend. If an ambulance is carrying a hurt person to the hospital, it does not have to stop for red lights or stop signs. The rule of stopping at a red light is ignored in order to save a person's life.

The Bible contains many rules for living. God gave us these rules to keep us happy, safe, and healthy. One of these rules is that we should remember the Sabbath Day to keep it holy. The seventh day of the week is a day to rest and remember all that God has done for us.

In Mark, chapter 3, the Bible tells how the Pharisees were watching Jesus and his disciples closely because they wanted to catch them doing something bad. They followed Jesus to the synagogue, a place where the Jews worshiped on the Sabbath. In that synagogue was a man with a deformed hand. Most people believed it was against the law for a doctor to heal someone on the Sabbath because this was thought of as work. The Pharisees wondered what Jesus would do. They watched him closely.

Jesus saw the man, and he knew it was important to heal the man's hand. Jesus knew that God made the Sabbath law in order to *help* people, not to keep them from doing good. So Jesus bent the rules and healed the man's hand. The person was more important than the rule.

It is important to follow rules, but sometimes it is more important to show love, to help someone who needs us.

Help us, dear Jesus, to follow rules that have been made to protect and help us. But show us that the most important rule is to love God and to love other people.

Notes

The Blame Game

Preparation: Bring a jar with enough cookies to distribute to the children at the end of your talk. (Optional) You might bring a giant foam hand with one pointing finger.

Would you like to play a game this morning? It's a kind of game that all of us have played before. It's called the "Blame Game." Let's pretend someone has stolen a cookie from my cookie jar. I will ask the first child on my right if he or she took the cookie. That person will say, "I didn't do it. He did it," and point to the next person. The next person will say, "Not me. She did it," and point to the next person. This will continue until the pointing comes all the way back to me. *(You may let the children point with the giant foam hand, passing it around as they go.)*

Have any of you played this game before? How many of you have gotten into a fight with a sibling or a friend at school and then tried to blame the fight on the other person? *(Children may share.)* I know I've blamed others before, and I've been blamed, too. Did you know that the "Blame Game" is very old? It goes way back in history to the very first people God created, way back to Adam and Eve.

God created Adam and Eve and placed them in a beautiful garden. The garden was full of good and beautiful things, and they were allowed to pick and eat almost anything they liked. There was only one rule; they could not touch the tree in the middle of the garden or eat any of its fruit. Along came the devil in the form of a serpent, and tempted Eve to try one of the fruits God had forbidden them to eat. Eve ate some of the fruit and offered it to Adam, and he ate some of it, too.

Did they both know it was wrong to do? Did they both know better than to eat from that tree? *(Let children answer.)* They both knew it was wrong, but they disobeyed. And then, when God caught them, Eve blamed the serpent. Adam blamed Eve, and he even blamed God. "But it was the woman *you gave me* who brought me the fruit" (Gen 3:12 NLT, author's emphasis).

The problem is, nobody wins in the "Blame Game." If you've done something wrong, you eventually have to admit it. And after you admit that *you* have done wrong, after you confess your sins to God, God will do something amazing. God will forgive your sins and erase the wrong that you have done. Blaming gets us nowhere, but asking God for forgiveness brings us peace and life.

Now, because nobody really did steal my cookies, I have plenty to share with everyone. Help yourself to a cookie before you go. *(Pass the cookies around.)*

Forgive us, Lord God, for the times when we disobey. Help us to not blame others but instead to go to you and ask your forgiveness.

Notes

Sprouting Kingdom Seeds

Preparation: Bring dry seeds in a glass jar, as well as seeds that have sprouted with visible roots and young shoots. Large, sprouted bean seeds work well for illustrating your talk; the roots and sprouts are easy to see.

T ake a look at the seeds I brought with me this morning. I'm storing them in this glass jar. I take them out every day to look at them, but they always look the same. I thought that maybe they should have leaves or roots by now, but nothing has happened. Why do you suppose that is? *(Let the children explain that you have to plant the seeds before they will grow.)* I have to plant the seeds?

You're right. A seed needs warmth and water to sprout. If I just leave these seeds in this dry jar, they'll never sprout, will they?

I have some other seeds with me, seeds that have been soaking in water. Do you see what has happened to these seeds? *(Show the children your sprouted seeds and let them comment.)* These seeds are changing, aren't they? They have the beginnings of little roots going down and a little sprout going up. Because these seeds were put into water, they had the chance to sprout.

Jesus explained many things to us by using picture stories or parables. He compared the kingdom of God to a seed. The seed must be planted in order to start sprouting and growing. Then it grows and grows on its own. Once a seed has sprouted, do you have to pull on its roots or help to stretch out its leaves and branches? *(Children may respond.)* No, of course not. The plant gets bigger even if no one is watching it.

When we tell people about Jesus, when we tell them that God loves them and that God sent Jesus to earth to show that love, it's like planting a kingdom seed. Our words may help to start that person's faith in God. Even though we help to introduce someone to Jesus, are we the ones who make their faith and trust in Jesus grow? No, God gives us faith, and God makes that faith grow.

It's always amazing to watch a plant grow. A tiny seed can become a huge plant. A mustard seed, which is as small as the head of a pin, can grow into a huge plant with strong branches where birds can rest and find shelter. We may not think that our own faith is very big, but just like the tiny mustard seed, with God's help, our faith will grow and grow into something big and strong that can help others.

Thank you for the gift of faith, dear Lord Jesus. Help us to plant seeds of your kingdom by introducing others to you, so that you can grow the faith in their lives as well.

Notes

What Do You Know?

D o any of you have questions that no one has been able to answer? Are there any really tough questions you would like to have answered? If you have one, go ahead and ask it now. I'm not going to try answering the questions, but I'd just like to hear them. *(Let children ask their questions.)*

(Give some examples of tough questions that you have encountered. My examples follow.) My kids have asked me tough questions, and sometimes I don't know how to answer them. When my son was about four years old, he asked me, "What makes gravity and what holds it down?" I didn't know the answer to that one. And after our pet rat, Tutu, died a year and a half ago, my daughter asked me what I thought rat heaven was like. I really didn't know how to answer that one either.

There are many questions that we *can* answer. We've learned a lot about this world we live in. But do you think there is anyone who can answer every question? We continue to discover more and more about this world. Scientists discover creatures that live way down deep in the ocean and don't need sunlight to live. People who study the stars and deep space discover new galaxies and places where bright stars are formed. There is already so much to know and to learn, and every day there is even more!

The book of Job in the Old Testament is about a man who had some tough questions, and he wanted answers. Why is there suffering? Why do bad things happen? He got many answers from people who thought they knew. But Job didn't believe their answers. In the end, Job realized that the real answers had to come from God. God is the one who created the world and the whole universe. Only God has all the answers. Some of our questions will have to wait until we get to heaven, but they will be answered.

Questions are very important. We learn by asking questions. God created us to be curious, to want to know. It's good to ask "Why?" I hope each of you will ask questions all through your life. Today during the service, think of a really tough question to ask your folks. If they don't know the answer, they may know someone you could ask or a book you could check. Or you might come up with a question that can't be answered yet. But keep asking anyway. You'll learn some amazing things.

Thank you, Creator God, for our incredible world and our curious minds. Help us always to seek out the true answers to our questions.

Notes

Get Up, Little Girl

Preparation: Bring an alarm clock with you as an illustration.

W hat time did you get up this morning? (*Let children answer.*) Did you get up by yourself, or did someone wake you up? Maybe you had an alarm clock, like the one I have here, to help you get ready for church on time. (*Show the children your alarm clock. You may even demonstrate how its alarm sounds.*) Sometimes if you're really tired and have trouble waking up, you might need someone to knock on your door or come into your room and shake you. Have any of you ever been so tired that someone has actually had to pull you out of bed and help you stand up on your feet? (*Let children share their experiences.*)

Did you know that Jesus once pulled someone out of bed and helped her stand on her feet? Yes, Jesus helped a twelve-year-old girl get up. You can find the story about it in the Gospel of Mark, chapter 5. But there was something very special about this story. This little girl couldn't be awakened by an alarm clock. She couldn't be awakened by a knock on the door. Her parents couldn't even shake her awake. No one could wake up this little girl, because she was in a deeper sleep than anyone here has ever experienced. This little girl was in the deep sleep of death.

At the beginning of the story, the little girl was very sick. Her father, Jairus, could see that she was dying, so he ran to get Jesus. He begged Jesus to come to his house and heal his daughter.

While Jesus was on his way to heal Jairus's daughter, a messenger came running up and told them that Jesus did not need to come anymore. The daughter had died. This did not bother Jesus; he told the father to trust him and kept walking to Jairus's house. Everyone was crying when they arrived. Jesus calmly told the people that the young girl was only sleeping. Some of those people made fun of Jesus when he said that, because they could see that the girl was dead. Jesus went to the girl's room, took her gently by the hand, and told her, "Get up, little girl" (Mark 5:41 NLT). And she got up, and she was alive and well.

Many of us have had someone take our hand and help us out of bed in the morning. Sometimes it's hard to get up, and we need help to step out of the world of sleep into the wide-awake world. When we reach the end of our lives and enter our last sleep here on earth, we know that Jesus will take our hand and help us step out of this world into heaven, where we will wake up to a wonderful life with him.

Dear Jesus, we thank you that you will be waiting for us at the end of our last sleep to pull us into the light and life of heaven.

Notes

A Nation of Rebels

Preparation: Bring two large, strong magnets that can be turned to attract or repel each other. Large bar magnets with clearly marked north and south poles should work well.

'd like to read to you from the Old Testament book of Ezekiel, chapter 2, verses 3-5. "'Son of man,' [God] said, 'I am sending you to the nation of Israel, a nation that is rebelling against me. . . . They are a hard-hearted and stubborn people. But I am sending you to say to them, 'This is what the Sovereign Lord says!' And whether they listen or not—for remember, they are rebels—at least they will know they have had a prophet among them" (NLT).

Did you hear the words *rebel* and *rebellious* in those verses? Does anyone here know what it means to rebel or to be rebellious? *(Let children respond.)* When you get to be teenagers you may know a little bit more about rebellion, but even young children sometimes rebel. To rebel means to turn against the one in charge or the one in authority. If children won't obey a parent and decide to go their own way, those children are rebelling. If students won't obey a teacher or if they refuse to listen in class and try to disturb others, those students are rebelling.

When someone rebels, it's like she is pushing against the grown-up who is trying to teach her. Let me show you what I mean by using these magnets. I can make one of these magnets "rebel" against the other by turning it so that the magnets push each other away. *(Demonstrate with the two* magnets.) When the forces of the magnets are turned against each other, it's impossible to get these magnets together. But if we turn the one magnet around, suddenly they come together very easily, almost as if they're hugging each other. It takes just one turn and the rebellion is gone.

The people of Israel were rebelling against God. They were pushing God away like magnets turned in the wrong direction. If they would repent or turn back toward God and start listening and obeying, what do you think would happen? (Let children speculate aloud.) It's just like when I turned the magnet around; the people of Israel would be pulled back close to God.

People sometimes turn against God and do bad things and try to push God away. But God always wants to pull us back to him; he wants to have a close friendship with us. The next time you feel like a rebellious magnet—pushing against your parents or your teachers or even God—remember to turn yourself around and let that push change into a hug.

Forgive us, Lord, for rebelling against you and sometimes pushing you away. Help us to change our direction and turn toward you again so that we can be close to you.

Notes

Career Change

Preparation (optional): You may bring paper and a marker to write down some careers that the children list during the sermon.

What do you want to be when you grow up? *(Let the children respond; you may write their ideas on the paper.)* Our ideas about what we want to do or be probably will change as we get older; but they may not. Some people decide at a very young age what they want to do as an adult, and that desire stays with them. They end up doing the very thing they had always planned on doing.

The Old Testament lesson today is from the book of Amos. Do you know what job Amos had? He was a herdsman and took care of cows all day. He made sure they had enough water and food, and he protected them from wild animals. He also was a tree trimmer. If there was a big tree growing next to somebody's house with a big branch hanging right over the roof, he might be asked to trim that branch back so that it wouldn't fall on the house and smash the roof. Do you think that's a job that you'd like to do?

Amos worked as a herdsman and a tree trimmer, but God had other plans for him. One day, God told Amos to go and speak God's messages to the people of Israel—to be a prophet. This was not Amos's idea. He never dreamed of being a prophet. A prophet told the people what God wanted them to do and how to live. It was a very important job. I'm sure that when Amos was standing out in the field with his cows he had no idea that one day he would be a prophet.

Amos had probably gotten used to being a herdsman and a tree trimmer. He might have been nervous about taking on the job of speaking God's words to the people. What if the people didn't listen and laughed at him? But God didn't let Amos down. He taught Amos what to say. God was with Amos the entire time, and Amos was a good prophet.

It's okay to make plans for our lives and to start thinking what we'd like to do when we get older. In fact, it's a very good thing. But sometimes, suddenly, God will change our plans. This change may be surprising; it may make us nervous or even scared. But you know, God's plans for us are always for good. And whatever it is God has for us to do, he will also show us how to do it and make us strong enough to do it.

No one can know for absolute certain what they're going to do when they grow up. But I know one thing for sure. Each one of you always will be a child of God. Even when you're all grown up, you'll still be a child of God. That will never change. And that is a very, very good thing to be.

Dear God, as we grow up, help us decide what jobs we will have. Help us to learn your will for our lives. Thank you that we will always be your children.

Notes

Sheep on the Lam

T he Gospel reading for today talks about sheep without a shepherd. Mark 6 says that when Jesus saw the
crowds of people who came to listen to him, he felt
sorry for them because they were like sheep without a
shepherd.

You may never have seen sheep without a shepherd, but
have any of you ever seen a child without a parent? A lost
child is a very sad thing. Have any of you ever gotten lost?
(Let children respond.) It can be very frightening to lose sight
of your parents when you're in a strange place and you don't
know where to go. You can feel scared and confused and not
know which way to turn or where to start looking for your
mom or dad. The best thing to do in that situation, of
course, is to stay put and wait for your parents to come back
and find you.

Kids usually pay attention and stay close to their parents,
or they yell for their parents if they get lost for a few
moments. But do you know what sheep tend to do when
they are without a shepherd to lead them? Sheep are not very
smart. They easily panic and run in circles; and if no one is
guiding them or leading them down a safe path, they have
been known to run straight off the edge of a cliff.

Sometimes there is trouble when a shepherd rounds up
his sheep at night to get them into pens. The sheep don't
understand that the pens are there to keep out danger, to
keep wolves from jumping in and eating them. They get
scared of the walls, and they run away from the place where
they would be safe.

And when a sheep runs away from its shepherd, do you know what you have? You have a sheep "on the lam." The expression "on the lam" means running away or escaping from something. A prisoner "on the lam" is one who's escaped from jail. A sheep on the lam is in big trouble. The sheep has no sense of direction, and it can't find its way home. It can't stop and ask for directions. It could run straight into trouble. The sheep may be free from the walls and the pen, but without the protection and guidance of the shepherd, it is in danger.

Jesus said that people are like sheep because sometimes people are just as foolish as sheep. We run away from God, or we turn away from rules that God gives us to keep us safe and protect us from evil. And when we run away from God and his loving care, we are like sheep without a shepherd. And that is a *baaaaad* thing to be. Even though sometimes we don't like rules, remember that God's rules are like walls that protect us and keep us safe.

Dear Jesus, thank you for being our Good Shepherd and giving us rules and boundaries to keep us safe. Help us listen to your voice and follow the good path that you lead us on.

Notes

Filling the Need

I f it was a hot day and I was really, really thirsty, what
would be the best thing for me: a chocolate milkshake or
a glass of water? *(Let children respond.)* I would need water.
After I had gotten my water, I might want a milkshake. But if
I were very thirsty, plain water would be the best thing for
me. What if I were starting school at a brand new place and
I was lonely: then what would I need? Would I need great
new clothes, or would I need to know all the answers on the
test, or would I need one good friend? *(Children can answer.)*
I would need a friend, wouldn't I?

Do you think God knows what we need? *(Discuss.)* God
knows everything about us. He knows how we feel, what we
think, and what we need. We can trust God to take care of all
our needs. Some things we may have to wait for. Some things
that we think we need may be just things we want. God is
good at sorting out those kinds of things.

One day, Jesus was near the Sea of Galilee and a huge
crowd of people came to hear him teach. It got to be quite
late—past suppertime—and everyone was getting hungry.
There were thousands of people. One small boy offered to
share his lunch; he had five loaves of bread and two fish.
Jesus took that small amount of food and started to pass it
around. And then a miracle happened: the little boy's lunch
was enough to feed everyone in the crowd. It wasn't fancy or
rich food, but it was what the crowd needed.

Usually, God provides what we need in ordinary, every-
day ways. But sometimes God surprises us with miracles that
show his power and wisdom. *(Here you may share your own*

story of God meeting a need in an ordinary or miraculous way. My example follows.) When I went to Trinity Lutheran College in Washington, my parents helped me pay some of the costs, and I earned some of the money by working at school. One spring, around Easter, I found that I did not have quite enough money to pay for that semester. I was about $80 short. I didn't know how I could raise the money in time, so I prayed about it. The next morning, while I was working as a receptionist at the front desk, an elderly couple, whom I did not know well, dropped off an Easter basket containing a large egg. They told me to keep the egg. It was very heavy and when I opened it up, I found that it was full of quarters and dollars! I counted the money, and it added up to $80. God had provided just what I needed!

God won't give us everything we want. We may sometimes want things that would not be good for us. But our Father in heaven knows what we *need*, and he will make sure that, somehow, we will receive those things that we truly need.

Thank you, Jesus, for giving us all the things we need. Help us trust you and not worry, because you will take care of us.

Notes

Hungry for Love

Preparation: Bring a loaf of bread that has been broken into pieces and placed in a basket for easy distribution.

I brought some bread in a basket this morning. I'll pass it around. You can help yourself to a piece of bread and then pass it to the next person. *(Pass the bread around; continue talking as the children help themselves.)* When we're hungry, we can eat bread and it satisfies our hunger. Now this doesn't happen very often, but once in a while we get so hungry that it hurts. And then even plain bread will taste good and it will stop our hunger. But if we eat this bread, will we get hungry again after a while? *(Let children respond.)* This bread doesn't keep us from getting hungry again sometime in the future.

Every day we get hungry, and we need food. Wouldn't it be great if food just fell from the sky and we could go out and collect it and then eat it? Do you know that actually happened once upon a time? Many, many years ago, God's people, the Israelites, were traveling through a desert with Moses. They didn't have enough to eat, and they got hungry and worried. So God sent bread from heaven. The people called that food "manna," which means "what is it?" Every morning they went out and collected the manna. There was just enough food for everyone every day. They didn't have to worry about being hungry any more.

Manna was bread God sent from heaven long ago. But do you know that God has sent us bread from heaven, too? Jesus is the true bread from heaven. Jesus said, "I am the

bread of life. No one who comes to me will ever be hungry again" (John 6:35 NLT). Jesus was not really talking about tummy hunger, but about heart hunger. People need spiritual food—the kind of love and care and goodness that God can give. When Jesus comes into their lives, they're never heart-hungry again.

Heart hunger is sort of hard to explain. How many of you have felt tummy hunger before? *(Children can raise their hands or talk about feeling hungry.)* How many of you have ever really needed a hug or a snuggle, or needed to hear someone say, "I love you"? *(Let children respond to your questions.)* That's heart hunger; it's like spiritual hunger. That kind of hunger can hurt even more than tummy hunger. With Jesus in our hearts, we know for sure that we are always loved. Jesus fills us up with his love and forgiveness and we're full. We're not hungry anymore.

Dear Jesus, Bread of life, thank you for filling us up and satisfying us with your love.

Notes

Burnt Anger

Preparation: Bring a clean cooking pot and a large spoon for pretending to stir. Also, if possible, bring along a pot that has a burned crust in the bottom.

I've brought something with me this morning. *(Show the pot.)* Can anyone tell me what this is used for? Do you have any of these in your kitchen? *(Let children tell what pots are used for.)* We cook food in these pots, don't we? You might put the ingredients for soup or chili in this pot, set it on the stove, and turn on the heat. After it's cooked for a while, it's ready to eat.

If you were going to cook something in this pot, what do you think you would make? Do we have any good cooks with us this morning? *(Children can share their ideas. You can use one of their culinary suggestions for the illustration, stirring the pot and pretending to cook as you talk.)* Let's say we make a pot of chili *(or other suggestion)*, and we put it on the stove to cook. It gets really hot and starts to boil. Then we turn down the heat, cover it, and let it simmer. After a couple of hours, we have a delicious pot of chili to eat.

What do you suppose would happen if we put the pot on the stove, turned up the heat, and then let it cook there all night? That would be a very dangerous thing to do, of course. Do you think the food would be any good to eat? It would be all dried up and burned to the bottom of the pot, wouldn't it? Do you think it's easy to clean a pot that's been sitting on the stove all night? It is really hard to get that burned crust out. Sometimes, it's impossible. You just simply have to throw the pot away. *(Here you may illustrate with the burned pot.)*

When we get angry, we're a lot like that pot on the stove. It's okay to get angry, but is it okay to get so angry we hit someone? No, it's not. Almost everyone gets angry with someone sometime. But is it all right to stay angry all day and all night and to keep that anger boiling like a pot on a stove? If you let anger simmer for too long, what do you think happens? *(Child may offer answer.)* If the anger cooks too long, it turns into burned anger and then it's really hard to get it out of your heart.

The Bible says, "Be angry but do not sin; do not let the sun go down on your anger, and give no opportunity to the devil" (Eph. 4:26 NLT). So the next time you're angry with someone and you feel yourself boiling over, what do you think you should do? Should you ask Jesus to give you enough love to forgive the person who has hurt you? *(Let children answer.)* It's better to take a pot off the stove before it burns, and it's better to get the anger out of our hearts before it hurts us and others.

Dear Jesus, help us never to let anger simmer too long. Take the anger out of our hearts and replace it with forgiveness and love.

Notes

Wisdom Bread

Preparation: Bring a loaf of bread to distribute among the children. You may package it in a bag labeled "Wisdom Bread."

Can anyone tell me what "wisdom" means? Can you make wisdom? Can you give someone else wisdom? *(Allow children to respond.)* Let me read some verses to you from the Bible book of Proverbs:

Wisdom has built her house, she has set up her seven pillars. . . .

She has sent out her maids to call from the highest places in the town,

"Whoever is simple, let him turn in here!"

To him who is without sense she says,

"Come and eat of my bread and drink of the wine I have mixed.

Leave simpleness, and live, and walk in the way of insight" (Prov. 1, 3–6 NLT).

The Bible talks about wisdom as if it were a woman who wants to help foolish people. She calls to those who don't have much sense to come into her house and eat "wisdom bread."

I brought some bread with me this morning. And, as you can see, it's called Wisdom Bread. Do you think that you'll become wise if you eat this bread? Not really. We can pretend. And by eating this bread we can show how much we'd like to put wisdom into ourselves. Everyone who would like to be wise can have a piece of this Wisdom Bread. *(Have a helper pass around the bread while you continue to talk and ask questions.)*

The opposite of wisdom is foolishness, isn't it? Do any of you ever do things that are foolish? I know I do. Can anyone think of something that would be foolish to do? *(Listen to the children's answers and respond to them, or give your own example.)* It would be foolish to poke a tiger with a stick, wouldn't it? The wise thing to do would be to keep your distance. It would be foolish to dive into the shallow end of a pool. You could bump your head on the bottom, or worse, you could break your neck. It would be foolish to start smoking cigarettes. Your lungs would fill up with gunk, and you might get cancer.

What do you think is the most foolish thing a person could possibly do? *(Let children give ideas.)* People do many foolish things. But the most foolish thing any of us could do is to turn our backs on God, to not believe in Jesus.

God loves the world so much that he sent his only son, Jesus, to save us from our sins and to bring us to heaven to be with him. It would be foolish to keep Jesus out of your life, wouldn't it? The wise thing to do would be to keep Jesus in your heart and stay close to God for the rest of your life. I pray that we will all live lives of wisdom, whether we have this wonderful wisdom bread or not.

Lord Jesus, come into our hearts to stay. Bring your love and wisdom into our lives.

Notes

Dodging the Arrows

Preparation: You might bring an arrow or a picture of a soldier's shield and armor to illustrate your talk.

Do you sometimes hear about wars that are being fought in our world today? *(Let children respond.)* It's always sad to hear that a war is going on somewhere, but wars have been fought for a long time. Even two thousand years ago, when Jesus was walking around here on earth, people were fighting wars. They didn't have guns, fighter jets, or bombs back then, but they did have other weapons that could hurt people.

Arrows were a weapon soldiers used long ago. If an army attacked a walled city, the city had archers stand along the top of its walls and shoot arrows down on the attacking soldiers. Sometimes the archers set their arrows on fire, and the soldiers down below would have to dodge fiery arrows.

If you were one of those soldiers below the city wall, you would have to run or jump out of the way to avoid being hit by an arrow. If you had a shield, you could hold it up to protect yourself. Back then, some shields were so big they covered you completely. A soldier would have a shield made for him that fit him perfectly. If arrows were zooming toward the soldier, he could step behind his shield and be protected.

There were other pieces of armor that a soldier could wear to protect himself. He could wear a wide belt to protect his stomach, an arrow-proof vest across his chest, and a metal helmet to protect his head. But a big shield was one piece of armor that could protect the soldier from head to toe.

There is a Bible verse in Ephesians, chapter 6, that talks about putting on every piece of God's armor to protect us against evil and the power of the devil. The Bible says, "In every battle you will need faith as your shield to stop the fiery arrows aimed at you by Satan" (v. 16 NLT).

What kind of fiery arrows do you think Satan tries to shoot at us? They are arrows that we can't see. They are things that can hurt our friendship with God and with other people. *(Let children discuss.)* Satan's "arrows" might be bad or angry thoughts that the devil tries to put into our heads. They might be temptations to take something that isn't ours. They might even be bad words that we suddenly feel like saying but know we shouldn't.

Those fiery arrows might sound scary, but remember that God has given each one of you a shield of faith. Believing in Jesus protects you. It protects you from harmful thoughts and actions. If you remain under the protection of the shield that Jesus gives, the arrows of Satan can never harm you. You are safe in the power of God.

Almighty God, thank you for protecting us from evil. Keep our faith shields strong.

Notes

Washing the Heart

Preparation: Bring a bowl of water, some soap, and a towel.

D
o any of you like to play in the dirt or make mud pies? *(Let children respond.)* Dirt can be lots of fun. And if there is water nearby, you can make mud pies and build towers and channels for the water.

But if you've been playing outside in the dirt and you're called in for supper, what do you need to do before sitting down to eat? *(Let children respond.)* We need to wash our hands, don't we? Why do we wash our hands? *(Discuss.)* If we eat with dirty hands, we might get sick. We might get dirt on the food as we pass it to others at the table, and they might get sick, too. Washing your hands before a meal is a good rule, isn't it?

A long time ago, before people knew about germs and bacteria and before they knew the scientific reasons for washing hands before eating, God made a rule for his people. He told the Israelites always to wash their hands before eating. This was a very good idea. God was trying to keep his people healthy. The Israelites followed that law long before they even knew why God had commanded it. They were still following it when Jesus was preaching here on earth.

If you have dirt on your hands, you can clean it off with soap and water. The germs get washed away along with the grime, and your hands are clean.

But if your hands aren't dirty, and you are thinking bad things—your *mind* is "dirty." Maybe you are thinking that

you'd really like to use your hands to slug your brother or to push your sister out of the way. If that happens to me and I want to free myself from those bad thoughts and actions, would soap and water help? Would it work to wash my hands in this bowl of water? *(Children can answer.)*

There's only one thing that can clean us from bad thoughts and actions and get rid of sin in our lives. Does anyone know what that is? *(Someone may answer.)* Because Jesus died on the cross for us, he has the power to forgive our sins and wash away all the bad things in our lives. And he promises always to do this for us. So when we are sorry and tell Jesus, he washes away our sin.

I'm going to pass this bowl of water around and let each of you dip your hands in. *(Pass around the bowl and towel.)* As you do this, remember that just as surely as soap and water wash your dirt away, Jesus washes away the sin from your lives. He makes us clean on the inside, which is even more important than being clean on the outside.

Wash our hearts and minds clean with your forgiveness, Lord Jesus. Thank you for saving us.

Notes

Faithful Acts

Have any of you ever gone to school and forgotten your lunch? *(Children may respond.)* I know I have. It's a terrible feeling. Lunchtime comes and your stomach growls. Then you have nothing to eat and no money to buy a lunch.

Now imagine that your friends come and sit down next to you and notice you have no lunch. Imagine that they shake their heads and say, "Well, I sure hope you find something to eat before the bell rings!" Does that help you very much? *(Let children answer.)* It's nice that they've noticed you and it sounds like they care about you, but if they don't share any food with you, are they really helping you?

Sometimes we hear about or see pictures of people who need our help. We may hear about local food pantries needing donations of food for hungry families. Our hearts may feel bad for those hungry families, and we want them to know how much we care. But if we don't try to help by donating food or money, then we don't give our hands a chance to follow what our hearts are telling us.

We also may hear about people who don't know Jesus. And our hearts may feel sad because those people can't tell how good it feels to know that God loves them. But if we don't tell them about God or invite them to church, they may never hear that Good News.

The Bible says in James, chapter 2, "Suppose you see a brother or sister [in Christ] who needs food or clothing, and you say, 'Well, goodbye and God bless you; stay warm and eat well'—but then you don't give that person any food or clothing. What good does that do? So you see, it isn't enough just to have faith. Faith that doesn't show itself by good deeds is no faith at all—it is dead and useless" (vv. 15-17 NLT).

It does matter that we feel love toward others and that we care about them. It's a very good and important thing to pray for others and to ask God that things get better for them. But if we don't also give some of our time and money and actions, then our faith may start to shrivel up and die. What do you think would make a person's hungry tummy stop growling—to tell them we hope they will soon get a wonderful feast or to hand them a healthy sandwich? *(Children can answer.)* What do you think would warm up a shivering person—to say, "I hope the weather gets warmer for you!" or to give them a jacket to wear? *(Discuss.)* What you do makes a big difference. You act your faith out in the things you do and say.

(Here you may wish to talk about a special offering or a community service that members, including children, can participate in. This also may be a time to recognize teachers who are giving their time and talents to help with Sunday school in the coming year.)

Dear God, may we actually do those things that we know we should do. Give us the strength and courage to do your will and show our love to one another.

Notes

Tongues of Fire

Preparation: Bring a small match and, if possible, a picture of a forest fire or burned buildings.

W ho can name some dangerous things—things to be careful of? *(Let children give answers; help them if necessary.)* Are tigers dangerous? Are lightning bolts dangerous? Some dangerous things are fairly large, and we can see they're dangerous just by looking at them. But some very small things are dangerous, too. I have something in my hand that could destroy a whole building. It could even destroy a whole city or a huge forest. *(Show children the match in your hand.)* This little match could start a very destructive fire.

I'm sure all of you know how dangerous it is to play with matches. Fire is not a toy to play with. You have to be very careful because a fire can get so huge so quickly that you can't control it. *(Here you may give an example of a recent destructive fire from the news or share one of your own experiences. My example follows.)* Some recent forest fires started with just a small blaze that quickly grew so big that fire fighters couldn't put them out or control them. Big fires get so hot that you can't even get close enough to throw water on them.

None of you is carrying a match in your pockets. That would be a silly and risky thing to do. But all of you are carrying something that can be even more dangerous than a match. I invite every one of you to stick out your tongue and look at it. *(Let children do this now.)* That tongue doesn't look very dangerous, does it? It may even look silly. But your tongue can cause so much damage. It can't burn down a building, but it can make someone else feel very sad. The things you say can really hurt people. And the older you get, and the better you get at using words, the more you can hurt others with your tongue. Words can make people so sad that they don't like themselves anymore.

The book of James in the Bible says, "The tongue is a small thing, but what enormous damage it can do. A tiny spark can set a great forest on fire. And the tongue is a flame of fire. It is full of wickedness that can ruin your whole life" (James 3:5-6 NLT). Did you know you were carrying around something so dangerous?

But we don't have to use our tongues for evil things; we can say wonderful and good things with our tongues. What are good things we could say to someone else? *(Let children give examples like, "I love you," and "Can I help?")* I hope that all of you will be careful with your tongues and always use them to help people and not hurt them.

Dear Lord, help us to learn to control our tongues. Help us always to use our voices to praise you, tell the truth, and help others with loving words.

Notes

Humble and Great

Preparation (optional): You may wish to bring a photograph of Olympic medalists standing on the awards platform.

How many of you have watched the Olympics? When they give out the medals—gold, silver, and bronze— which medal-winner gets to stand on the highest platform? *(Let the children answer.)* The highest platforms are for the top prizewinners, the athletes who won the gold medals. *(You may show your photo here.)* Gold-medal winners also get to see the flag of their country raised up higher than the other flags as the band plays their national anthem. It's wonderful to see how happy those winning athletes are.

One day, the disciples of Jesus were holding their own kind of Olympics. They were arguing about which one of them was the greatest. Can you imagine Jesus' own disciples doing that? It seems pretty silly doesn't it? When Jesus asked them what they were arguing about, they wouldn't answer him. Jesus knew, of course, so he told his disciples, "Anyone who wants to be the first must take last place and be the servant of everyone else" (Mark 9:35 NLT). To the disciples, it must have seemed like Jesus had turned everything upside down. The highest was the lowest, and the lowly servant was on the very top getting the gold medal.

If we tried to figure out who was the greatest among all of the children up here this morning, like Jesus' disciples did among themselves, we might ask questions like: "Who is the fastest runner?" or "Who has the best toys?" But to be great in the kingdom of God, we don't have to be the fastest or the richest. To be great in God's eyes, we have to be humble and loving. Being humble means not thinking that we are better than others. Being humble means letting others have their way and being ready to be kind and helpful to others.

If we used Jesus' method, we wouldn't ever try to figure out who was "best." Instead, we would look at ourselves and ask questions like: "Can I help my parents clean the floors this morning?" or "How can I make my brother or sister feel happy about themselves?"

It might be hard to ask ourselves questions like these. We all like to do things that seem important and that make people think we're "winners." When we watch the Olympics or other sporting events, it's easy to get the idea that the winners are the ones who come in first, who are better than others. But God wants us to remember that the humble servants are really the winners in his kingdom. We are at our very best when we are serving others.

Dear Lord, give us a humble spirit and make our hands always ready to serve others. Help us remember that putting others first is better than being first.

Notes

Praying with God

Preparation: A good illustration for this talk is a portable CD or cassette player with a familiar song ready to play.

How many of you sing in a choir? Raise your hands. Do you enjoy singing with other people? What do you like about it? *(A volunteer may respond.)* What would it sound like if a choir got up to sing, and one section started to sing "Happy Birthday," a second section sang "Jesus Loves Me," and a third section sang "Twinkle, Twinkle, Little Star"? *(Children can answer.)* That would just be a confused noise. A choir has to sing together with parts and music that all fit together.

Let's see what happens if we try to listen to one song while we sing another. *(Here you may play your recorded song while you lead the children in singing a completely different song. Make sure the recorded song is loud enough to compete with the voices of the children.)*

That did not sound very good. Those two songs didn't really go together. They clashed with each other, and it was hard to sing our song while listening to a different one.

How many of you pray to God? Raise your hands. A lot of us pray to God, but I wonder how many of us pray *with* God. Praying can be like singing in a choir. If we are praying with God, our voices work together, and the prayer is a beautiful and powerful thing. When we are just praying *to* God, we might be just asking and asking God for things we want. When we pray *with* God, we are also listening carefully for what God can tell us, for what God wants us to know and wants us to have. For example, we might pray to God for a motorized scooter, but God really wants us to run and walk more in order to make our bodies stronger. Or we might pray to God that a bully would disappear from our lives while God really wants to help us turn that bully into a friend.

The Bible says, "The earnest prayer of a righteous person has great power and wonderful results" (James 5:16 NLT). A righteous person is one who tries to know what Jesus wants. When a righteous person prays, she is listening for God's voice, for God's words, and praying right along with God. And that person begins to understand what God wants her to pray for. Amazing things begin to take place.

So even though it's tempting to kneel down and ask God for everything we want to have, even better things can happen if we try praying *with* God. Pretend that you and God are singing in a choir together, and before you ask for something, listen carefully to what God might be saying. Find out what God wants to give you and what God wants to do with your life. Then jump right in and start praying for those things.

Teach us to listen to your voice, dear Lord. Help us to pray with you; not just to you.

Notes

Let the Children Come

Preparation (optional): You may bring along a "welcome" mat or sign from your home.

D oes anyone know what the word "welcome" means? You sometimes see the word on a mat in front of a door. Or you might see a sign along the road that reads "Welcome to Minnesota" or "Welcome to the Dew Drop Inn." *(You may pass around your own welcome sign.)* A welcome sign is a good thing to see, especially if you're looking for a place to stay.

There are some places where a child might not be welcome. You might not be allowed into a scientific laboratory where there are expensive test tubes and machines. If you bumped into a table you might set off an explosion. If you were in Washington, D.C., you probably wouldn't be allowed to walk right into the president's office. Children, and even adults, aren't always welcome in every place.

What are some places where you are always welcome? *(Children may offer answers.)* You are always welcome in your own home. You are welcome in your school. You are welcome in the church. Who are some people who always welcome you with open arms when they see you? *(Let children share.)* Moms and dads, grandmas and grandpas, and best friends all welcome you when they see you.

And all of you are sitting in a place where you are welcome to come. When it's children's time during the church service, we get to gather up here and talk to each other and learn about God. All the children in church are welcome up here with us. And once upon a time, long ago, there was another important children's time when little boys and girls were welcomed to come up and learn about God. It happened while Jesus was preaching and teaching on the earth.

One day, parents brought their little children to Jesus so that he could bless them. But Jesus' disciples tried to send the children away. They thought Jesus was too busy for these children. Jesus told his disciples: "Let the children come to me. Don't stop them! For the Kingdom of God belongs to such as these" (Mark 10:14 NLT). Children like you are always, always welcome in the arms of Jesus. He is never too busy for you. He is always waiting to hear your prayers and to welcome you into his kingdom. Children's time is a wonderful reminder to all of us that Jesus welcomed and blessed children. Jesus said, "Let the children come to me."

Remember that Jesus wants children to come to him. Children have a special place in God's heart. You never have to wait to talk to Jesus. He's always ready to listen to you and to welcome you.

Thank you, Lord, that all of your children are always welcome in your embrace.

Notes

The Eye of a Needle

Preparation: Bring a large backpack stuffed with things. Place a chair at the front where everyone can see it. You (or a volunteer) will attempt to crawl under the chair—first with and then without the backpack. You should be able to do it when you remove the pack. Also bring a large needle.

Today I brought a big backpack stuffed full of things that I own. *(Show the children the backpack you're wearing.)* It's very bulky. I'm going to pretend I'm on a hike and need to crawl under a fence. We'll say this chair is the fence. Do you think I'll be able to do it? Let's try. *(Attempt an unsuccessful crawl under the chair with the backpack on.)* Looks like I'm not going to get under. How do you suppose I might be able to get under the chair? *(Let children give suggestions.)* Take off my backpack? You're right, it is the only way. I just can't take all this stuff with me. *(Take pack off and crawl through the space.)* Well, I made it that time. Thanks for helping.

The space under that chair is pretty small, but is it as small as the eye of a needle? *(Show the needle and let the children answer.)* The eye of a needle is a tiny space, isn't it? Do you know what Jesus once said? He said that it is easier for a camel to go through the eye of a needle than for a rich person to enter the kingdom of God.

Jesus meant that it might be difficult for a rich man to enter God's kingdom if he loved his riches too much. This does not mean it's impossible for rich people to enter God's kingdom, but they have to love God more than their riches.

Sitting on the Rainbow

The Gospel lesson for today tells about how a rich man ran up to Jesus and asked how to make it into heaven. This man was very nice, and he had tried hard to obey God's commandments ever since he was a child. But Jesus could see into this man's heart, and he knew there was a problem. The man loved his money and his things more than he loved God.

Jesus looked lovingly into that man's eyes and told him what he needed to do. "You lack only one thing," said Jesus, "Go and sell all you have, and give the money to the poor, and you will have treasure in heaven. Then come, follow me" (Mark 10:21 NLT). The man could not do it. All of his riches were too important to him. He walked away from Jesus.

Jesus' disciples were shocked when they heard what he told the rich man. "Then who in the world can be saved?" they asked. And Jesus answered, "With people, it is impossible; but not with God. All things are possible with God" (Mark 10:26-27 author's paraphrase). It's easy to think about and love our things more often than we think about God. God can help us make him most important in our lives. We only need to let him.

God, help us to love you more than anything in this world.

Notes

The Greatest

Preparation (optional): Bring in a low stool that you can cover with a rich-looking robe or piece of fabric.

This morning I'd like to set up a royal kingdom here. I'll need a king, queen, princes, princesses, dukes, and duchesses. And I'll need a servant to wait on all the royal people. Are there any volunteers to be in our royal court?

(Choose volunteers for the royal titles. Using the child's own name, announce their roles: King Alec, Queen Laura, Princess Elsa, etc. Have the children stand in a line at the front of the church with the king and queen at one end. Announce each member of the royal court with appropriate pomposity.)

We have a very fine court here this morning. We have a king, a queen, princes, princesses, dukes, and duchesses. Do you know what we're missing? We need a servant to wait on all of these important people. Will someone volunteer to be the lowly servant? *(Wait for a volunteer or, if necessary, choose a likely candidate from the "royals" to stand at the end of the line.)*

Can someone tell me, in the eyes of God, who of all these people is the greatest? Is the king the greatest? Is one of the dukes the greatest? *(Wait for answers.)* In the eyes of the Lord, the servant is greatest of all. I'd like for our servant to come up here to the top step to stand above everyone. *(Have the servant come to the top step at the front of the church or provide a stool draped with a rich-looking cloth for the servant to step onto.)* In God's kingdom, the lowliest servant is the greatest.

Could the entire royal court, including any lowly servants, come and sit down again? I have something I'd like to read to you. These verses are from the book of Mark, chapter 10. Two of Jesus' disciples, James and John, wanted to be very important people in heaven. They wanted to sit right next to Jesus by his heavenly throne. The other disciples grew angry with them. Why should James and John have the best seats? So Jesus had to explain something to them.

"Whoever wants to be great must be a lowly servant," Jesus explained, "and whoever wants to be first must be a slave of all. For the Son of Man also came not to be served but to serve, and to give his life as a payment for many" (vv. 43-45 author's paraphrase).

Jesus is the Almighty King, but he didn't come to earth to demand that people serve him. Jesus came to be a servant to all and to give up his life, so that we might have eternal life.

I hope that all of you will become great in God's kingdom by serving others with all of your heart!

Dear Jesus, thank you for leaving your throne in heaven to come here to earth as a servant. Help us to be servants in your kingdom by serving those around us.

Notes

Wishbone

Preparation: Bring a wishbone to pull and break with one of the children.

What is this little thing I'm holding? Can someone tell me? *(Hold up the wishbone and let the children explain what it is and what people do with it.)* It's a wishbone, isn't it? Why is it called a wishbone? Two people take hold of the bone—one on either end—and they each make a wish. Then they pull until the bone breaks apart. The person left with the bigger piece gets his or her wish.

Who wants to make a wish and pull the wishbone with me? *(Choose a volunteer. Then close your eyes, make a wish, and break the wishbone together.)* Now, do you think the person with the bigger piece will really get his or her wish? *(Let children respond.)*

What's the difference between wishing for something with a wishbone and praying to God for something? Which one is more certain of coming true? Which one do you have more faith in? *(Let children offer their answers.)*

Pulling a wishbone is not like praying to God, is it? But sometimes it can seem important. I can remember fights over wishbones and wishes. Sometimes wishbone wishes can seem like they're worth a lot, even worth yelling about.

During Bible times, a blind man named Bartimaeus was very certain that his wish would come true. He wanted his blind eyes to be healed; he wanted to be able to see. As soon as he heard that Jesus of Nazareth was coming his way, he

Sitting on the Rainbow

knew he would finally get his sight. He had faith in Jesus, and soon everyone around him knew about his faith because he began shouting, "Jesus, Son of David, have mercy on me!" (Mark 10:47 NLT).

Bartimaeus shouted at the top of his lungs. He may not have been able to see, but he certainly was able to speak. He used his voice so loudly that the people near him were embarrassed and tried to get him to be quiet. But Bartimaeus would not be quiet. More than anything, he wanted to be able to see. And he knew that more than anyone in the world, Jesus had the power to grant his wish. So he yelled for Jesus. And Jesus heard him and told him to come. Bartimaeus ran to Jesus' side and Jesus gave him his sight. "Go your way," said Jesus, "Your faith has made you well" (Mark 10:52 NLT).

It's fun to make wishes with wishbones or to wish on the first evening star or on birthday candles we've blown out. But when it comes to counting on someone—being absolutely certain of something—it's important to put our faith in the One who will never fail us. Put your faith in Jesus.

Jesus, make our faith strong and help us pray to you with a faith like blind Bartimaeus. Open our eyes to the power of your love.

Notes

The Important Things

Preparation: Bring a small stuffed animal that can represent your pet. Make a large fancy sign displaying the name of your pet.

How many of you own a pet of some kind? *(Let the children share some information about their pets.)* Do you love your pet and take care of it? It is important to take care of your pet because it depends on you for food and shelter. But it especially needs love and care from you.

I brought a stuffed animal with me today to represent my pet. Let's pretend this is my real pet because I want to show you how much I love my pet. I'll just set my pet over here while I show you my great love for my pet. I love my pet so much that I have a big sign with his name on it. *(Show the sign and give all your attention to the sign, but none to the pet.)* I love this sign that I made for my pet.

Everyone who comes over gets to see this sign! Isn't it great? Sometimes I hug this sign. I keep it with me all the time. Do you think that I am a good pet owner? *(The children can comment.)* I'm paying more attention to this silly sign than I am to my pet!

Jesus once talked to some people who were acting almost as silly as I am with my sign. They had a lot of rules in their church (or synagogue) and they got so caught up in following and loving those rules, that they forgot about the most important thing: they forgot about loving God. Jesus was asked which rule was the most important and he answered, "You must love the Lord your God with all your heart, all your soul, all your mind, and all your strength." And then Jesus added, "The second is equally important: Love your neighbor as yourself" (Mark 12:30-31 NLT).

I got distracted by a fancy sign and forgot all about my little pet. There it sits, lonely and ignored. I'd better pick up my pet and give it some hugs and attention. *(Pick up your stuffed animal pet and snuggle with it.)* That makes more sense than hugging a sign with the pet's name on it, doesn't it?

In the same way that I ignored my pet, sometimes we get distracted by other things and forget about loving God and our neighbors. Is loving God and loving those around us more important than dressing up for church? *(Let children respond.)*

God wants to be the most loved thing in our lives. And God wants us to love each other. We show our pets love by petting them and giving them attention. We show our love to God by praising him. We show our love to others by treating them with love and kindness. Love God and love others; those are the most important things.

Dear Lord God, help us to remember the most important things in life. Help us to love you more than anything else and to love our neighbors as much as we love ourselves.

Notes

Tiny Big Gift

Preparation: Bring two bags containing stickers or some other kind of prize or treat. One bag should contain just a few items, the other, many items. Have extra items yourself to give to the helper with the meager prize-bag.

I have two bags of prizes with me this morning. I'd like two volunteers to help me hand them out. *(Pick your helpers and give them each a bag.)* As you can see, one of the bags is fuller than the other. I'd like my helpers to start handing out prizes. They have to take turns, though, as they hand out their prizes. First one person will give out a prize, then the other person will give out a prize until everybody has been given a prize. Then, after everybody has gotten a prize, these two helpers get to keep for themselves whatever is left in their bags. We can help by counting as they hand them out. *(Let the volunteers begin. Try to make sure that the one with the meager bag has few or no prizes left when finished.)* Does everyone have a prize?

Which one of these two helpers gave out the most prizes? *(Let children respond.)* They handed out about the same number, didn't they? But one has very few prizes left and the other still has a bag full. So they may have handed out the same number, but which of these two do you think was the more generous? *(Children may answer.)* The one with just a few prizes to begin with gave away almost all that she had. The one with lots of prizes still has plenty left. *(Give your extra prizes to the helper with the empty bag. Then have the two helpers sit down with the rest of the children.)*

Something like this happened when Jesus and his disciples were sitting at the temple, watching people drop their money in the offering box. As they watched the crowds come by, they saw many rich people put in large amounts of money. It was an impressive offering the rich people gave. Then along came a poor widow. She put just a small amount into the box. But Jesus saw her, and he said to his disciples, "This poor widow has given more than all the others have given. For they have given a tiny part of their surplus, but she, poor as she is, has given everything she has" (Mark 12:43-44 NLT).

When we give our offerings of money or time or talent to God, he doesn't compare our offerings to those of other people. Some of us have more time or more money than others to begin with. God looks at what we have to start with, and God looks at the attitude we have about giving. When we give with a generous and thankful heart as much as we possibly can, God is very pleased and happy.

Lord Jesus, help us be generous in sharing all the gifts that came from you in the first place.

Notes

Through the Curtain

Preparation: Bring a lightweight piece of material that can be torn in half easily—an old sheet, for example. You may want to cut one edge slightly in the center of the cloth, so it will be easier to tear. If you can do so, drape the sheet over a rack or high chair so it blocks the altar from the view of the children.

A long time ago, the Israelites worshiped God in a church called a tabernacle. The tabernacle had a walkway around the outside and several large rooms inside. At the very center of the tabernacle was a place called the Holy of Holies. That was a small room that had a very thick curtain closing off the door. The only person allowed into the Holy of Holies was the high priest. Nobody else could go behind the curtain because that was the powerful presence of the Almighty God.

In those long-ago times, before God sent Jesus to us, people did not go directly to God with their offerings and sacrifices. The high priest would take their offerings to God, and he would receive messages from God for the people. The high priest was the only one who could meet God behind the curtain in the Holy of Holies.

The Israelites knew that God was very, very powerful and holy. They knew that they were very sinful and not at all holy. And they were even afraid to be near God's special holy room. Before he went into the Holy of Holies, the high priest had to clean himself carefully and wear special clothing and put away any unclean or bad thoughts.

The high priest's robes were trimmed with bells, and a rope was tied around his ankle. When he entered the Holy of Holies, the other priests would wait outside. They were not allowed to go in. If anything happened to the high priest and if they heard him fall, the other priests could drag him out with the rope. They would not dare go inside themselves.

When Jesus died on the cross for our sins, do you know what happened to the curtain that covered the entrance to the Holy of Holies? *(Allow children to respond.)* The thick curtain was ripped from top to bottom, just as easily as this thin material is torn. *(Tear the piece of sheet so children can now see the altar behind it.)* Jesus' death opened a doorway to the presence of God. Now we never need to be afraid to go to God ourselves. We can come with our prayers and our offerings at any time.

The book of Hebrews, chapter 10, says, "Now we are sure that we can approach God by the blood of Jesus, by the new and living way that he opened for us through the curtain, that is, through his flesh" (v. 19 author's paraphrase). Because Jesus died for us, we can approach the Almighty God.

We thank you, Lord, for opening a way for us to talk to you and for bringing us through the curtain into your awesome presence.

Notes

A Solid Throne

Preparation: Bring a chair that slides or rolls easily across the floor to serve as a throne. Place it where the children will be able to push it for some distance.

Today is Christ the King Sunday. Did you know that? Today we read Bible verses and sing hymns that remind us that the Lord is King over everything on earth and in heaven. How do you recognize a king? *(Children can offer responses. You may prompt them with more specific questions.)* What does a king wear? A crown, a robe. What does a king hold in his hand? A scepter. What does a king sit on? A throne.

Let's pretend just for a bit that I'm a king and this chair here is my royal throne. I'm going to sit down; then you try to move my throne. Go ahead and push on my throne. Does it move? *(Let children push the chair so that it slides a little.)* My throne is not very solid and strong, is it? Is it made of heavy stone? Is it bolted to the floor? No. It can be moved very easily. That's not surprising, though, because I'm not really a king. In fact, this is not really a throne.

Who is really a king? Who is our king? *(Let children answer.)* Let me read to you from Psalm 93 in the Old Testament: "The Lord is king! He is robed in majesty. Indeed the Lord is robed in majesty and armed with strength. The world is firmly established; it cannot be shaken. Your throne, O Lord, has been established from time immemorial" (vv. 1-2 NLT).

Is God's throne solid? Can it be moved? Can God's kingdom ever be taken over by some other king? *(Let children*

Sitting on the Rainbow

respond.) No, it can't. God's throne is even more solid than the earth! If you jump up and down on the earth, can you move it? (*You can try jumping with the children.*) The earth seems pretty solid, doesn't it? But even the earth moves sometimes. There are earthquakes and volcanoes and land that gets washed away into the sea. God's throne is stronger and more solid than the very earth that we're standing on.

There have been many kings and queens who have lived at different times and in different lands. Some of them have wanted to rule the whole world. Some kings and queens have been very powerful and have taken over many countries. They have built huge, beautiful castles and have had fancy thrones. But when those rulers of this earth reach the end of their lives, are they kings and queens anymore? No. Usually another ruler takes over their throne.

The kings of this earth don't compare to our heavenly King who rules over everything in heaven and on earth. God's kingdom has no end. It is a kingdom of love. And we are part of that kingdom. Thanks be to God!

Thank you, Lord, for being the eternal King over the earth and the heavens. All glory and honor be to you, Lord God.

Notes